RON DE BOER

Questions from the Pickle Jar

Teens and Sex

The Office of Abuse Prevention of the Christian Reformed Church
and Faith Alive Christian Resources
Grand Rapids, Michigan

Questions from the Pickle Jar: Teens and Sex by Ron DeBoer is a copublishing venture of The Office of Abuse Prevention of the Christian Reformed Church and Faith Alive Christian Resources.

We welcome your comments. Call us at 1-800-333-8300 or e-mail us at editors@faithaliveresources.org.

Library of Congress Cataloging-in-Publication Data

DeBoer, Ron
  Questions from the pickle jar: teens and sex / Ron DeBoer
      p. cm.
   ISBN 978-1-59255-298-6
1. Christian teenagers—Sexual behavior. 2. Sex—Religious aspects—Christianity. I. Title.
BT708.D43 2008
241'.66—dc22

2008029138

10 9 8 7 6 5 4 3 2 1

Table of Contents

Preface

Have you ever camped outside an arena waiting to buy concert tickets? Or stood in a line that stretched three city blocks for the chance to score tickets for the playoffs? Maybe you and a couple hundred of your closest friends have huddled outside in the early morning frost with blankets and hot chocolate, waiting for Best Buy to release the latest electronic gadget you just had to have.

Why would you and lots of other people go to such lengths for a concert ticket or the newest X-Box game? The answer is simple. Because that something is important to you. If you want something bad enough, you will stand in long lines, in the cold, at odd hours.

Four years ago, a small group of people decided that talking with young adults about healthy sexuality is important too. Young adults are our children, our grandchildren, our family members, our neighbors.

What motivated this small group was our concern that a healthy view of sexuality *wasn't* being talked about. Some young adults experienced child abuse, which distorts how people view their bodies and sexuality. Others told us that conversations about sex were taboo—no one seemed willing to talking about it. And lots of people turned to Hollywood or the Internet to guide their thoughts about sexuality.

So this small group huddled over coffee, tea, and early drafts of this material for hours on end. We wondered if we had thought of everything. We wondered if it would connect with you, the reader. We agonized; we prayed; we drank more coffee; we asked for more drafts.

And now we're happy this book is finally ready for your eyes and for your hearts. We wish you happy, healthy lives in service to God, your family, and your community.

—The small group

The members of the small group are Mary VanderVennen, Lori Keen, Jack Vos, Brian DeKraker, Gerry Heyboer, and Beth Swagman. And with thanks for the countless hours and discussions on healthy teen sexuality, the small group acknowledges Shaun and Andrea Hofing, Gayla Postma, and Bill Veenstra.

Introduction

Charlotte was my first girlfriend. She and I were in fifth grade together, and one of the many things I remember about her was that she smelled like licorice. The first day I saw Charlotte, my heart did a drum solo. She stepped up onto the school bus in slow motion and made her way down the aisle, her hair blowing mysteriously, the way it does in a shampoo commercial, as she slowly scanned the seats. When our eyes met, she smiled, revealing a straight row of silver braces. I felt like Peter Parker when he first lays eyes on MJ in *Spiderman*. I would have climbed a wall for her that day.

I thought about her every night after that. I'd never had a girlfriend before and was freaked out that a girl could make me feel that way inside. A *girl!* For some reason, I asked Charlotte to "go with" me. That meant she would sit next to me on the bus as it rattled and bounced over the country roads to our school. One afternoon, several days into our relationship, she kissed me on the cheek before she ran off the bus as it arrived at the end of her driveway. I felt tainted and dreamy all at once. I fell asleep that night, certain we'd one day be married.

Charlotte, though, had a different idea. She broke up with me the very next day. I felt like Bart Simpson when his girlfriend rips his heart out of his cartoon chest and drop-kicks it against the wall. Sure, eventually there would be other girlfriends. But I remember none of them with the clarity of the day Charlotte flashed her silver smile and introduced me to the Land of the Opposite Sex.

Adam must have felt that same charge of electricity the first time he laid eyes on Eve. Picture it. There he was, all by his lonesome, moping around with animals and caring for plants. Until one day he falls asleep, wakes up with a sore side and—whoa!—who's this magnificent creature in the garden? Rubbing the sleep from his eyes, he approaches Eve, smiling at this person who *kind of* looks like him but with new, enhanced features he's never noticed in his own reflection in the pond. Needless to say, he probably got a little excited. You might not think this is a big deal but remember, fig leaves weren't in fashion yet. What followed had to have been like the courtship between Bambi and Faline in the Disney classic you watched when you were a kid—the two of them all batty-eyed and giggly.

The Bible doesn't tell us much about Adam and Eve's life together before their fall into sin, but I imagine they must have had a blast together in the garden. It must have been like one big all-inclusive vacation when time stood still. Between running with tigers and watering flowers, Adam and Eve probably held hands and gazed into one another's eyes, too, slow dancing to the night-time chorus of frogs. No doubt they hugged each other during storms, laughed at each other's jokes, and teased each other the way any young couple might. Their relationship, you'll remember, was created by God's hand—it was perfect in every way, the model for boyfriends and girlfriends leaning against lockers in every school hallway in North America. Adam and Eve trusted, respected, and protected each other. They were honest with each other. We don't actually see any of this in Genesis, and the last time I checked there's no Paradise footage on YouTube, but we do know theirs was a *perfect* relationship.

Since God told them to be fruitful and multiply, they probably spent a lot of time having sex too. Why not? They didn't need a minister to marry them. They were created by God to be in union with one another from the get-go. Besides, they had a great big world to populate.

You know what's cool? Adam and Eve figured out how to love each other—body, soul, and mind—and maintain a relationship without check-ing out *Honeymoons for Dummies* from the library or watching Dr. Phil every afternoon at four.

Unfortunately, between moonlit strolls, Adam and Eve sinned. You've probably heard that story a hundred times. Their honeymoon ended as abruptly as a weekend courtship on class camping trip. They turned on each other—and they lied to God. Enter the fig leaves. Adam and Eve covered themselves up, no longer comfortable with their nakedness. This covering up was a symbol of the effect sin had on all of life. Sin changed everything for Adam and Eve, including their sexuality. Their relationship —and every relationship after that—would never be the same. Sex, which began as a beautiful, God-created way for a man and a woman to express their love for each other, became something shameful because of sin. It became something to be hidden.

Here we are thousands of years later, and we're still keeping it hidden.

Do you talk about sex with your parents? I sure didn't. I don't know about you, but I had a hard time even saying the word *sex* when I was a teenager. In my household, sex was only acknowledged when the dog got a bit frisky or someone was naughty on a sitcom. (By *acknowledged* I mean everyone got all fidgety and our parents smacked the dog or made us turn off the TV.)

Despite our lack of formal education on the subject of sex, my brothers and I still managed to use words like *humped* and *wang* and *hooters*. How did we learn these words, and why were they always dirty? Everyone was aware of the subject of sex and had a mittful of words describing every aspect of the act, but nobody treated the topic with respect.

Guys might have accused each other of playing pocket pool, and girls might have stuffed their bras to make themselves look womanly, but no one learned the nitty-gritty about sex. For instance, I don't remember the word *masturbation* ever appearing on a spelling list. My only sex education in junior high took place when my gym teacher held up a pencil-drawn picture of a naked man and one of a naked woman and laid them on top of one another. "That's how babies are made," he said. "Now, anyone feel like badminton?"

In early high school we sat through films of teenage boys having wet dreams or girls as the victims of date rape. We knew we were supposed to take these topics seriously, but we mostly laughed at the kids in these films—their funny hairstyles and outdated clothes.

The truth is, we all desperately wanted to learn more about the inner workings of sex. Today anyone can Google this stuff and get some answers; back then, we had no idea of the difference between fact and fiction. "Does every other guy really have a larger penis than mine?" we wondered. "Do other girls let their boyfriends inside their shirts?" Unless you had an ultra-cool mother or father who actually talked about these things, you wandered the media for sexual context or listened carefully to older kids for clues to the secret world of sex and relationships.

What about you? Do you wonder about this whole business of sex and relationships? Do you wonder if you're not normal because you're studying for your college SATs and you've never had a boyfriend? Has your view of sex been formed by *American Pie 14* or *Girls Gone Wild* clips on the Internet?

If you're a Christian teen, you may have looked in the Bible for answers. If you read the Song of Songs, for instance, you'll find some heavy-duty poetry about love and intimacy. Take chapter 3, verse 1: "All night long on my bed I looked for the one my heart loves; I looked for him but did not find him." Pretty steamy stuff! Or how about chapter 4: "How beautiful you are, my darling! Oh, how beautiful! Your eyes behind your veil are doves. Your hair is like a flock of goats descending from the hills of Gilead." Okay, up until the part about the flock of goats, this would be a great poem to write on red heart-shaped construction paper. Solomon, the author of Song of Songs, must have been one romantic guy.

You want to hear something really cool? A footnote in my Bible says that Solomon wrote the entire book of Song of Songs "to affirm the sanctity of marriage and to picture God's love for his people." Yeah, that's a bit of a mouthful. I mean, who uses the word *sanctity* anymore? But it means the *purity* of marriage, the *cleanliness* of marriage, the *spotlessness* of marriage. In the 1 Corinthians, Paul has this to say about sex and love: "We must not pursue the kind of sex that avoids commitment and intimacy, leaving us more lonely than ever—the kind of sex that can never 'become one'" (6:17, *The Message*).

Do you see a common theme here? Sex and intimacy are gifts from God best celebrated within the boundaries God sets for us. Does that mean you must feel guilty for having sexual thoughts that just pop into your head or for fantasizing about that hottie in math class? *Au contraire*. Anything you're feeling, anything you're imagining, any question you have about sex is 100 percent normal. Did I mention you shouldn't feel guilty about your thoughts? Your mother probably had the same thoughts—OK, that went way over the line.

Whenever I taught sex education in high school, I always did the questions-in-a-jar schtick. Maybe you know it. Kids could scrawl any question they wanted answered on a scrap of paper and drop it in this pickle jar. Then I would spend two or three periods pulling out questions and unlocking the secrets to erections and ovaries.

When I answered the questions, you'd have thought we were in a library, it was so quiet. *Everyone* wanted to know the answers to those questions. This surprised me. And it taught me that lots of teens pretend to know everything there is to know about sex. The reality is most teens don't know everything, and what they do know comes from some highly questionable sources. In fact, nobody knows all the answers about sex and relationships—not even me, even though I had lots of girlfriends.

Think of this book as a pickle jar. All of your questions about sex and relationships won't be answered, of course, and you may already know 83.7 percent of the answers to the questions on the scraps of paper I've pulled out in these pages. But I hope there will be a few things in the book that get you thinking about this awesome, scary, exciting topic of sex and relationships.

So let's talk about sex . . . the way God intends it.

CHAPTER 1
Who's in Your Top Ten?

Sorry about that long introduction! Once I get started you can't shut me up. The fact that you are still reading tells me one of two things: (a) your mom or dad or youth leader is making you read this; or (b) you want to learn more. I'm hoping for (b).

I'm guessing you've found a nice, safe place to read—maybe the attic, or maybe your bedroom. So make yourself comfortable. Enjoy the book. If you disagree with parts of it, you can yell at the book. It has a stiff spine. If you like what you read, hug the book. (Every time you hug a book, the author gets a warm fuzzy feeling.)

OK, here we are in your bedroom. I'll bet somewhere in your room you have pictures of your friends and family, maybe even your pit bull. Go ahead, look at them right now. If you've got a computer in your room, I'll bet you could go all Mozart on your keyboard right now and pull up a thousand pictures of your friends on your personal web pages. Am I wrong? (You'd think I've known you for years, wouldn't you?)

Let me ask you something. Why do you have so many pictures of your friends and family? Go ahead, look away from the book and try to answer the question. (Don't answer out loud—your parents will think you're hiding someone in here.) Let me hazard a guess . . . because you care about these smiling, goofy people—and they care about you too, right? You care about them so much you put your head against theirs, snapped a shot on your digital, and made a collage.

Perhaps there are a few people on your walls you *really* care about—like your best friend, a teammate, or your third cousin Lenny. And I'm guessing there might be a face you keep glancing at that makes your heart leap. Go ahead, look at that picture right now.

This book will eventually get to the heavy-duty relationships—such as the boyfriend-girlfriend tandem—and even marriage, the mother of all relationships. But for now, let's just think about all the great relationships you've had and still have at this point. Think about all the different people you invite into your life. You'd probably describe each one differently, wouldn't you? Try it. Write down all the people you have a relationship with right now, and beside each name, try to describe the relationship or at least how you feel about the person.

Here's how my list would have started back when I had peach fuzz on my chin:

My father	Strict; sometimes fun; my biggest Christian role model; love being with him watching sports; someone I can't really be honest with.
My girlfriend, Karen	I get all short-breathy when I'm alone with her in her basement; I care about her more than anyone. She's funny and way smarter than me in school.
My best buddy, Doug	He makes me laugh; we understand each other without even talking; I'd stick up for him in a fight.
My teacher, Mr. Schat	I like being around him; he makes me feel important; he has lots of wisdom; I listen to his opinion of things more than anyone's.

Go ahead, make your own list. Maybe you'll want to limit your list to your top ten relationships—you know, the David Letterman thing. (OK, if you're feeling really popular this week, write down as many names as you can—even the janitor at school who says "howdy" to you every morning as he wet-mops around you while you're trying to pull your math book out of your locker.)

Either you cheated and skipped your assignment or you're back already. Either way is cool by me. It's *your* bedroom. If you listed the people who are important to you, you probably learned as much about yourself as you did about them. I wonder what everyone who would list *you* on their chart would write about you. Would it be the same as what you wrote about your relationship with them? Hmmmm. That's the kind of deep stuff you share around a campfire with your youth group while everyone stares at the logs or pretends they have smoke in their eyes.

The point is, you have a ton of different kinds of relationships. And you will continue to have lots of relationships throughout your life—hopefully long after you get hitched or become an astronaut or whatever. What you want to remember is that in all your relationships, God wants you to be *honest* and *respectful* and *loving*. These concepts comprise some of the boundaries God sets for us.

You might be wondering, "How can I be loving to the guys on my football team or the girls at school?" As you know, love can look like a lot of things, but the Bible says it simply and perfectly: "Love your neighbor as yourself." And by neighbor, it doesn't just mean old Mrs. Higgins who lives next door and owns thirteen cats. It's the dude in your math class, the guy who makes the fries at the fast food joint where you work, the girl sitting beside you at youth group.

Remember Solomon, the king who asked God for wisdom when he got his one wish? He sure had a lot of good things to say about our relationships. In Proverbs 13:20, he says "Walk with the wise and become wise; for a companion of fools suffers harm." I don't know about you, but I've hung around with some real boneheads in my time—guys I thought were funny and courageous because they "didn't take nothin' from nobody." They were rude to teachers, didn't respect girls, and mouthed off at their parents. In short, they ignored the relationship boundaries God sets for all of us. I realize now it felt really safe to hang around with guys like that—I didn't have to do anything except sit around and cut people up. Maybe you've had similar relationships.

Here's another assignment. Go down your list again and put a little "w" beside the name of each person you think is wise. Do the same with an "f" if there are any fools on that list—people you hang with who aren't wholesome, don't respect other kids, don't love God, make poor decisions that seem kind of fun but you know are wrong. (Don't worry, I won't make you show them.) Would you be labeled a fool on anyone else's list? Time to stare into the campfire again! See you in a bit.

OK, next question. You might want to go get a bowl of ice cream before this one. In all those pictures on your wall or on your personal web page, is there anyone of the opposite sex who you're thinking you might want to get kinda serious with, maybe even spend the rest of your days with, share the toothpaste with, fight over the remote with, snuggle with when thunder rolls and rain beats against your bedroom window? Don't be shy. There *is* someone, isn't there? Yes or no, write your answer right here: _____.

If you said no, skip the next three paragraphs. You're safe for now—but you might want to stick a piece of uncooked spaghetti in this spot for future reference when the person who will one day grin all goofy-like with you at the front of the church comes stumbling into your life.

If you said yes . . . wow, you're thinking about marriage already. Maybe you already know *when* you and your "friend" are going to get married. My then girlfriend and now wife, Karen, and I knew in high school when we were getting married, but we didn't tell anyone. It was one of those little secret treasure chests only she and I had the key to. We talked about it at our favorite abandoned parking lot. Later, when we got engaged, we didn't get married for another two-and-a-half years. (Man, it was hard getting through that long engagement and not having sex!)

The Bible has a lot to say about married people. Genesis says God created man and woman to be together, to be joined in a lifelong union. "For this reason a man will leave his father and mother and be united to his wife, and they will become one flesh" (2:24). Yeah . . . except I didn't really leave my mother and father after I got married. I was still in college and we actually had to move in with my parents for two months before we got a place of our own. Can you say "awkward"?

Even Jesus talked about marriage. He told those Pharisees who were always stalking him, "The Creator originally made man and woman for each other . . ." (remember Adam's hubba hubba reaction when Eve showed up at Eden?). "Because God created this organic union of the two sexes, no one should desecrate his art by cutting them apart" (Matthew 19:4-6, *The Message*). His art? I probably wouldn't call myself a work of art, but my marriage is, that's for sure. In fact, marriage is like this big painting on a canvas where the artist is constantly working away. The work is never done; it's continuously evolving and changing. Sorry, I didn't mean to get all Rembrandt on you there, but you catch my meaning, right? You don't stand in front of the minister, go for an all-inclusive honeymoon somewhere, and everything is hunky-dory until your fiftieth anniversary. Marriage takes work. Just ask my wife.

If you're a "no" person, congratulations. Here is your "Normal" bumper sticker. For those special people like *moi* who already knew the babe in senior English would one day share a wedding photo frame with me, you have to know, we are *not* normal. Some high school relationships do end up in marriage, but most of them don't make it to the sexennial—just so you know, that means *sixth*—anniversary.

If marriage isn't even on your Doppler radar, I salute you. You are living your life with all the goofballs on your bedroom collage and personal web page. You text your buds every day and LOL with an entire table full of people in your school cafeteria without a worry in the world about what your boyfriend or girlfriend is thinking. That's called being a teen.

But you need to know that out there somewhere you probably have a soulmate who is looking for you. Your eyes will meet, and fireworks will go off sooner or later. You will know who this is by the sudden deep breathing you will find your lungs doing. Eventually, I'm going to be talking about marriage and sex (do *not* put the book down!), but you don't have to be doing either of the two to be reading about it. When the fireworks go off, you will have read the part about sex and marriage and you will be ready. You might even tell your future life partner you have read the book on sex and marriage and are ready for your first date. My advice: don't mention the book. Just go bowling or something.

CHAPTER 2
(Your) Relationship Timeline

Hey, reader. Welcome to chapter 2. Did you write your name in the title? This is *your* chapter. Let's call it your own personal iChapter. No one else will read it unless you decide you want to show people. This is between you and, well, *you*, I guess.

You're actually going to do most of the writing in this chapter. It might seem kind of weird to you that the writer would ask you to contribute a chapter to his book. Let me explain. This book is about you. It's written to help you figure out some of the stuff you might be experiencing, stuff like sex and relationships.

In this chapter, I would like you to write down your sex and relationship timeline. You're probably thinking, What the heck is *that*, writer? Well, a sex and relationship timeline (let's call it a SART so I don't use so much ink) is a list of the things you've observed, heard about, or even done in relation to sex and relationships with members of the opposite sex.

I know, I know, you've probably never talked to anyone of the opposite sex *that way*, let alone been touched by one of them. (Hmmmmm!) But I know you've *thought* about it a bit. You can't tell me you haven't. I also predict you probably know quite a bit about sex and relationships. Go on, admit it. You've seen pictures on the Internet and in magazines. You've heard about stuff from your friends on instant messaging. You may have even had a "Charlotte" (remember . . . my first girlfriend) experience on a bus somewhere.

Here's what I want you to do. Go back as far as you can and try to write down all those "aha" moments when something dawned on you or happened to you that has anything to do with sex and relationships. Now I know this could possibly be very sensitive to you, so I don't want to make light of it. If that's way too hard for you because of things that have happened to you or things you've seen that hurt way too much to visit right now, then feel free to jump right to the next chapter, or maybe talk about it with someone you trust.

Here's *why* I'm asking you to write down your SART. First, I think it's important for you to realize that you do in fact have a sex and relationship history—so you won't assume half of the stuff in this book doesn't apply to you.

Second, I think it's important to write this down because truths you never knew were even inside you will emerge the minute you start jabbing away at the computer keys or applying pen to paper. When you start writing, things come out that you may have long suppressed. If you've ever written in a journal or sat around a campfire with a bunch of people talking about deep subjects such as why the sky is blue or why whales have to die, you'll know what I mean. If you've never written in a journal or talked around a campfire and you don't know what the heck I'm talking about, then this is your first trust-the-voice-in-your-head exercise. I wouldn't ask you to do something if I didn't think it was important.

Now I'm not a teacher who throws out an impossible writing assignment to the class, then sits at the back of the room clipping toenails or reading the sports section while *you* labor over the assignment. I am going to show you my own personal SART from preschool through age eighteen, so you have a model to use. That's right, the voice in my head is going to get all George Washington honest with you. Some of this stuff is kind of personal, but if I'm asking you to write down some personal stuff then I should too, right? After all, you've invited me into your house. The least I can do is be honest with you.

OK, here goes. I've split my chart into three columns. The first column gives my approximate age at the time of the "aha" moment, the second describes what I observed, and the third tells what I learned.

Age	What happened	What I learned
5	Saw my parents holding hands while walking around Niagara Falls on a family outing.	People who love each other hold hands. My mother and father often modeled affection to my brothers and me. It was always clean and loving.
6	First-grade parents night at school. The mom of one of my classmates (she couldn't have been more than twenty-one), arrived in tight blue jean shorts, a low-cut top, and blue eye shadow. She was snapping gum.	Some moms were cool. Also, people who dress like that are hussies because that's what my parents called my classmate's mother on the way home that night. I learned that how someone dressed reflected how they felt about sex (at least that's the message I got).
7	In second grade, a girl named Dee Dee chased me around the classroom—and outside at recess every day—because she wanted to kiss me. My mother phoned the school to complain when I tattled on Dee Dee.	I learned that some girls liked to kiss boys. A few years later, Dee Dee died in a house fire and my mother told me her father was very mean to her when she was little. I didn't know until I was a teenager that "mean" meant she had been abused. I still feel guilty for ratting on her. She was acting out the only thing she knew.
7	When my younger brother and I were at a park, a man exposed himself to us and was touching his "thing." Being the older brother, I hustled my little brother away and found our parents. We didn't tell them what we had seen though.	I thought I had seen a man going to the bathroom. I now know different. That I didn't say anything means one of two things: I was too embarrassed; or I feared my parents would get mad at *us* for seeing this guy. (Later in the book, I will talk about sexual abuse in its many forms.)
8	In third grade I sent a note via my friend Steve to a girl named Jodie Ann while our class was in the library, telling her I liked her. Steve returned with her answer: I really *bugged* her.	Love hurts. Jodie Ann was my first crush. I put myself in a vulnerable situation sending that note—and I got burned. I was scared to approach any girl after that. After Jodie Ann, every girl, including my wife, had to make the first move to get my attention. We are affected very early in our relationships with the opposite sex.

8	In third grade I had two TV crushes. One was Samantha Stevens, the mother on the situation comedy *Bewitched*. The other was Ann Romano, the mother on the situation comedy *One Day at a Time*. Needless to say this feeling of lust towards two *mothers* was alarming to me.	You never know what it is about a person you will fall in love with. These two mothers had qualities I liked—warmth, smiles, and a bit of naughtiness—in a motherly sort of way, of course. (I'm sure Sigmund Freud would have had a term for this.) Later when the TV show *Charlie's Angels* came out, all my friends went gaga over Farah Fawcett Majors and Jaclyn Smith. I liked Kate Jackson—"the smart one." I took a lot of abuse for that one. Love wasn't just about a hot body to me—even at a young age. Was I weird or what?
10	At school a girl named Tracy threatened to phone me at my house. I told her she'd be too chicken. When she did call, I was changing out of my school clothes. I grabbed the phone thinking it was my buddy, Dave. Instead, Tracy's voice breathed into my ear—while I was in my underwear! I was filled with very weird feelings of disgust and embarrassment, as if she could see me.	Even at a young age, when sex wasn't even part of my vocabulary, I knew there was an embarrassing connection between talking to a girl and being in my underwear. Nobody had to teach me that "Spiderman briefs" and "girl" was an awkward combination.
11	In fifth grade a boy named Paul taught the guys every dirty word there was to know. By the end of September, I knew all the words there are about the female body—from top to bottom. Paul proceeded to call us these words whenever we played soccer.	There was something dirty about girls' bodies. These strange, exciting words had sparkle, but I knew intuitively they were wrong. I, in turn, taught my younger brother all the words, and one day, he asked our mother what the c--- word meant. By age eleven I knew sex and naked bodies were very bad things.
11	My first girlfriend, Charlotte. See the Introduction for more details.	I had strong feelings toward Charlotte, most notably that she smelled like licorice. Odors are not the foundation for a good relationship.

11	In the fifth grade, I was flipping through the channels of our TV and came across a naked woman dancing around a pole. It was there and gone within two seconds. The TV program was a documentary about the prostitution problem in Vancouver. Those were the first breasts I had ever seen—of the bouncy variety, I mean. The jolt of excitement/guilt I felt was very confusing.	There was a mysterious side to sex that I had never seen before. I didn't understand the documentary or the context of the TV show, but the image of the woman affected me in a way I didn't yet recognize. I hate the word "aroused" so I won't use it. I was excited when I saw that video and thought about it for a long time. I was surprised to find myself flipping through channels looking for similar glimpses in the days that followed.
12	Not quite a teenager, I found an adult magazine—a "Playboy book," as we called them. The rush of feelings that immediately seized my body when I flipped through the magazine surprised and shocked me. If the TV documentary was a thunderbolt, these pictures brought on a tsunami of feelings. I hid the magazine under a rock and retrieved it a few days later and hid it in an old tackle box in my bedroom closet where it stayed for months—until my mother found it!	My knowledge of the female body and of sex leaped from words and stories to graphic pictures of adults doing things I didn't think were possible. I was physically excited, of course, but didn't know what the response really meant. I was also very bothered and couldn't look at a woman the same way knowing what was "down there" and "behind there." I truly believed this was the way women behaved when they were alone in their houses. I also learned more about the "dirtiness" of sex. My father said my mother had been upset for days after she found the magazine. (I will talk more about pornography later in this book.)
13	In the locker room at the YMCA, my seventeen-year-old brother took off his suit after a swim, revealing his pubic hair. I was shocked and embarrassed. I looked away. Was I going to get that tangle of hair "down there" some day?	My body was going to change. I remember my brother's body when we were younger—it didn't look like *that*. I grew more and more introverted about sexuality. At age thirteen no one, and I mean *no one*, had talked about any of this with me.

14	A girl named Amanda held a spell over me as a high school freshman. Everyone wanted to go out with her. But she wanted to go out with *me*. She even broke up with her previous boyfriend in front of me, then waited for me to ask her to "go with" me. Remember Jodie Ann from third grade? I was afraid of rejection so I never asked Amanda out even though we had many alone times after school and at each other's houses as friends. Eventually some other guy did.	This was true love. We were teenagers and in high school. Everybody was pairing off. But I was scared. "Going with her" wasn't holding each other's hands stuff. It meant being alone together, making out, telling personal things to each other. It also meant fighting, making up, and eventually breaking up, which I witnessed in all my friends' relationships. I just wanted to play basketball. I was too passive and I lost the girl I was secretly in love with—but nobody knew, not even her.
14	Truth or dare at a high school freshman party. I had to make out with a girl named Rachael. It was the first time I had kissed longer than two seconds. Rachael went at it pretty good, using her lips and tongue in a way that made me freeze. I mimicked her behavior without knowing what the heck I was doing.	This girl-guy thing was really serious. I didn't like kissing like this at all. It wasn't sport to me. I would only kiss someone like that if I was waaaay in love with her. I avoided all parties involving guys and girls until sophomore year.
16	Still no steady girlfriend. Mostly my thoughts about sex were in two categories: (1) the rude, funny stuff I shared with friends (mother jokes and lusting after girls while driving around town in my buddy Dave's VW Rabbit); (2) the images and information sought out in the media. I stayed up late on Friday nights to catch the off-color shows like *Benny Hill* and movies on the foreign station.	I learned as I hit my mid-teens that sex and relationships between men and women were more than hand-holding and nice weddings. I learned it was easier to keep it at a distance—laugh at it and indulge in thoughts about it privately. No risk. No worry.

17	A very good high school friend in my peer group became pregnant. We were all shocked for weeks. Literally numbed. We had joked about sex. We had learned about it in health. We had watched scenes in movies. But none of us was actually having sexual intercourse. Our friend was, though—obviously.	This was one of those coming-of-age incidents that literally threw my friends and me—both girls and guys—off the cliff into the valley of adulthood. One of our own not only had had sex but was going to be a parent. This reality scared me even more.
18	A girl was rumored to like me. Everywhere I went, she happened to be there. I'd known her for years—we had been in many of the same classes. In our senior year, I was student council president; she was student council vice president. We found ourselves planning school events and fundraisers together. At a hockey game, she asked me to "squish" her to keep her warm. Finally, I got the message (remember my Jodie Ann experience!). I asked her on a date only because Karen's best friend told me she'd say yes if I did. She said yes. We went to a movie then sat in a restaurant and talked for about four hours, laughing and drinking coffee until 1:00 a.m. When I finally took her home, I got her grounded for a week for breaking curfew. We didn't care. Fireworks went off that night.	There was nothing about sex in my date with this girl. Our night out was one of talking and laughing—just the way I had imagined relationships when I was five and watched my parents holding hands. The making out and physical exploration would prove to be a natural progression (more on that later) but we started out as best friends with shared interests and we continue to have that relationship well into our married life. We take seriously the core expectations God has for us—respect, honesty, and unconditional love.

Whew. That took a little longer than I thought it would. There are many details I didn't include, of course. I could probably write a book and include a lot of graphic details, but you'd be too grossed out by that. Let's do this one step at a time. I have to tell you something. When I told my friends I was going to get honest with *you*, they were like, "Why would you want to tell someone you can't even see about your personal sex and relationship experiences? Aren't you afraid it will fall into the wrong hands?" I was like, "How can I ask teenagers to be honest about their stories if I'm not honest about mine?"

I have a feeling it will be a lot easier for you to be honest with yourself about, say, masturbation, when you know that 99 percent of guys and girls have done it. If I had told you, "Good Christian teenagers do not touch themselves . . . down there . . . and if they do they will probably go to hell," you'd be putting this book back on the library bookshelf so fast you'd probably get a "shhhhh" from the librarian.

Now, I'm not saying you should go all 1960s and do whatever feels good without thinking about what you are doing and why you are doing it. That's not the purpose of this book. The purpose of this book is first to be honest with each other, and then to give a solid Christian perspective on the whole topic of sex and relationships by considering God's boundaries and expectations for our relationships. After all, we are Christians, right? I don't know about you, but when I was your age, I wish there had been a book out there written by someone who was willing to be honest about what he went through as a teen. The best I got was a hardcover textbook with a Picasso-style stick boy and girl on the front.

Now, if you are a girl, you might be thinking, "What is this guy going to tell *me* about what *I'm* feeling?" I understand where you're coming from. That's why I'm asking my wife all kinds of stuff about what it was like to be a teenage girl. She wasn't a cheerleader or anything, but she was a pretty normal teenage girl who had boyfriends, did her homework, and worked part time at Burger King. That's also why, when I dive into some of the topics such as abuse and boyfriend/girlfriend power struggles and "what a girl wants" issues, I will split up my thoughts specifically to guys and girls.

OK, it's time for you to get out some lined paper or log onto your computer and write down your own sex and relationship timeline. See you in chapter 3.

CHAPTER 3

Sex and the Media

Hey, reader. Glad you came back. You know, I've got to get something off my chest. Let me tell you what happened. I was sitting at my desk, writing this book, trying to decide in what order I should talk about sex and relationships when I decided to take a little break, shake some chips into a bowl, pour myself a nice frothy glass of cream soda, and settle in front of the TV for a while.

It was a Friday night. I clicked on the TV and—whammo—I'm hit between the eyes with a woman having an orgasm while washing her hair. Maybe you've seen that commercial too. Why does washing your hair have to be a sexual experience? It diminishes this beautiful, wonderful thing God created. As I started channel surfing, I couldn't help but notice that pretty much everything on TV is charged with sex with no hint of the boundaries and expectations God sets for sex and relationships. Honesty, respect, and love are sorely missing. Sex is purely physical. I catch a couple of videos on MTV and I get a screen full of bodies flaunting their charms. I settle into a sitcom, and soon enough someone is coaxing someone else out of their clothes. What the *heck!*

I began to yell at my TV. I would have thrown my chips at it, but I was hungry. My wife ran down the stairs to see if I had fallen into the dryer again but stopped dead in her tracks when she saw me shaking my finger at a Coors Light commercial. She turned off the TV, slowly guided me by the elbow back up the stairs, and tucked me in bed.

But here it is the next afternoon, and I want to share with you, reader, a letter I wrote to the media this morning. I'm just about to lick the envelope and send it off.

Dear Media,

I am writing to you on behalf of Christians all over North America who are sick and tired of the confusing messages you send to us every day. Have you no sense of right and wrong? We happen to think sex is something beautiful between a man and woman in a marriage. You'd have us believe we're morons if we haven't slept with someone by the time we're sixteen.

You, TV. Listen up. Every night, you try to convince me that if I buy a Ford Mustang, a beautiful blond will want to have sex with me. Or that somehow drinking beer will turn women on. You give us TV shows in which everyone wants to have sex. What's up with that? If you do have married couples in your shows, they are desperate house-wives looking for the next plumber to drop his tool belt. Even your so-called reality shows are all about sex and cheating and break-ups.

But you know what's really confusing, TV? After all these shows about teens having sex or mixing alcohol with relationships, you show us the news where we hear about kids drinking and driving, and programs for teen moms who are trying to finish high school while raising the two-year-old who was born in their sophomore year. I've got news for you, TV. You are setting up a culture where teens having sex is normal. Then you shake your head in judg-ment at those same teens when they do. That's wrong.

Well, guess what, TV? Lots of teens aren't having sex. They're waiting until they get married before they do what your char-acters are doing every Tuesday night at nine o'clock. Lots of teens adhere to the expectations God has established for us.

So here's an idea: create a show that reflects the wonder-ful gift of relationships and sex God has given us and that focuses on characters who demonstrate respect, honesty, good communication, and unconditional love.

And you, magazines. Don't think you're getting off easy.

Do you really think that when I'm standing in line at the grocery store I believe the women on your covers are real? I know all about airbrushing and computer enhancement. Do you think a bit of cleavage is going to seduce me into dropping a fiver so I can take you home? Come on. I'm not stupid. I haven't come across a cover girl at church or at the video store. Why are you trying to convince girls and boys that real beauty comes in a five-foot-ten-inch, one hundred fifteen-pound body? Don't you know you're conditioning guys and gals to think anything else is ugly? And why place so much emphasis on looks, anyway?

Try being creative for once. Try doing a cover on a woman's sense of humor or her intelligence. The kind of woman I want to fall in love with has to love God, and she doesn't need D cups and ivory white teeth to do that.

Hey, Internet. I consider you the back alley of the media. You've got more seedy streets than New York City. Don't you feel just a teeny bit guilty that because of you, ten-year-old boys can watch people having sex? How can you sleep at night when you pour every conceivable distortion and abuse of sex right into people's houses? You should be arrested. Don't you know that the billion or so guys who stare at pornography for hours every day suffer in their relationships with real women? How can you portray women as objects of men's sexual desires? If it weren't for e-mail and YouTube, I'd unplug you forever.

Yo, video games. Yeah, don't stand there looking all innocent. I know you like to hide behind slick packages with bright colors. I know, I know, you produce lots of educational stuff for children, but what about that Grand Theft Auto 27? Encouraging kids at the controls to identify with a character who shoots people and has sex with prostitutes is disgusting. Do you not care that these same boys will one day be asking girls on dates, and the only media relationships they've seen involve violent sex? You should be locked away with TV and Internet.

Media, I would like to encourage you to go back to some "traditional values" in your programming. We're not prudes, but when you show ultra-cool teens in ultra-cool clothes having sex, I get confused. I see it so often I begin to think everyone must be doing it. Please show some teenagers whose relationships exemplify respect, honesty, and love—and who wait until they're married to have sex. Like I said, there are lots of them.

Anyway, thanks for reading my letter. If you'd like me to appear on CNN or in *Time* with some of my ideas, feel free to give me a call.

Sincerely,

Ron DeBoer

The truth is, we get a lot of our knowledge about sex and relationships from the media. And let's face it, the commercials are pretty funny, the TV shows are well-crafted, and the magazines are pretty alluring. I know what you're thinking . . . just because you watch a season of *Desperate Housewives* doesn't mean you're going to want to have sex after the junior prom. Maybe you're right.

But when you watch TV shows that celebrate sex outside of marriage, read magazines that deliver a message about "real" beauty, watch MTV, which is actually more about sexual images and body language than it is about music—without you even knowing it, sex will become routine. When sex becomes normalized, it loses its intended, special place. It becomes recreational, something to be randomly given away with those who come and go from your life instead of an amazing gift to share with someone you make a vow of love to in front of your church.

Despite all the messages you see, all the images you digest daily, remember this: God wants our relationships to be about more than just sex. Sex between two people is intended for marriage only. Karen and I thank God often for the circumstances leading up to our going out that first night. We became best friends who love each other to the core. We celebrated our mutual interests and supported one another. We waited to have sex until we got married.

Was it easy? Is it easy for a kid who's left all alone in a room with a bowl of ice cream to refrain from eating it? *No, it was not easy!* Every message in the media taunted us to go ahead and do it. We were getting married anyway, right?

The reality is you can make as many justifications as you like to give yourself permission to have sex with your boyfriend or girlfriend. The real challenge for you will be to work on respect, honesty, and good communication. These qualities—not great sex—make great relationships.

So go ahead—write your own letter to the media if you want. It feels good.

CHAPTER 4

A Touchy Subject

Remember that pickle jar I talked about in the Introduction? Whenever "DeBoer's Pickle Jar Days" arrived on the health class calendar and students got a chance to write down any question to which they needed an answer, there were always several inquires about masturbation. Is it wrong? Is doing it after every meal OK? Do girls masturbate as often as boys—or at all? Should Christian teens masturbate?

OK, that last question never got asked, but I'll bet you've asked yourself that question. Or it might have been more like, "Is God going to smite me because I masturbated tonight?" (Don't you love the word *smite?* You're talking all-out obliteration when you say *smite.*) I know during my teenage years I thought I'd be punished with zits and seventeen plagues if I did it.

It's funny what guilt will make you think. I used to think we each had a certain number of orgasms in store for us—like we are born with a certain number of bullets in the chamber—and that once we got married, boy, would we be sorry when we ran out. But I'm sure you already know that for guys, the body is constantly reloading and there's no fear of ever running out. And for girls, there is a lifetime of good feelings locked inside you.

So let's be clear. That great feeling we get is a gift from God. Come on, admit it. Few things in life feel as good—not even the feeling you get when you first bite into your favorite candy bar or guzzle a Coke after a basketball game. Those don't even come close.

Masturbation is one of those words that's rarely spoken out loud. I'll bet you've said it more times in your head since you started reading this chapter than you have out loud to other people in your whole life. In this chapter, we're going to pull some masturbation questions out of the pickle jar.

But first, a brief, unofficial history. Masturbation has probably been around since the beginning of humankind. Depictions of male masturbation are relatively common in art from the ancient world. While masturbation may have been practiced over time, it has been taboo for hundreds of years. In 1758, a Swiss doctor named Tissot published an article saying masturbation was one of the causes of mental illness.

About a hundred years later, another doctor, Sylvester Graham, said that loss of semen in males was injurious to health. (He also said married people should have sex only twelve times a year!) To reduce cravings to masturbate, Dr. Graham recommended that teens should eat mild, wholesome foods (such as the Graham crackers he invented). I'm not kidding about this stuff! One of Graham's followers was Dr. John Harvey Kellogg, who created Corn Flakes to curtail children's inclinations to masturbate. (Google it and you'll find the proof. In fact, Kellogg had all kinds of ideas to keep teens' hands off themselves—for girls, he believed the application of pure carbolic acid to their sexual parts was an excellent means of getting rid of any abnormal excitement. Ouch!)

Did you know that between 1856 and 1919, the U.S. Patent office granted patents for forty-nine anti-masturbation devices? Thirty-five were for horses; fourteen for humans. The human devices, made for boys, consisted of either sharp points turned inward to jab the penis should the boy get an erection during the night, or an electrical system to deliver shocks. I'm crossing my legs as I write! How many of these devices were actually used, or what effect they had on the children, no one knows. Masturbation by girls was considered even more shocking, shameful, and unmentionable.

Early Christians believed masturbation was wrong, even though there is no mention of the practice in the Bible. Some Christians believe that the story of Onan of Judah, who "spilled his semen" rather than procreate with his brother's widow, Tamar, as was the Jewish custom (Genesis 38), refers to masturbation. But most biblical scholars believe Onan did have intercourse with Tamar but "withdrew" so she would not become pregnant. So repeat after me: there's no mention of masturbation in the Bible.

34

Psychologists today say masturbation is a good way to relieve tension, but as it is one of the least-talked-about subjects in sex education, most teens still feel guilty when they masturbate, and most adults are still reluctant to say it's OK. Despite all this, you should know that teens have been masturbating since ancient times, so if you're one of them, you're not alone.

And now to the pickle jar. I'm pulling out the first question.

Does everyone masturbate?
Most teen boys have masturbated by the time they are sixteen. According to health experts, about 75 percent of girls have masturbated at least once by the time they turn eighteen.

Will masturbating too much hurt me somehow?
Masturbation cannot hurt you. Some teens think that if they masturbate too much their sexual organs will stop working—kind of like a lawnmower wears out if you cut too many lawns. This is not the case. Masturbation is about what your brain is telling your body parts. Your body parts will respond if your brain is convincing enough.

If I masturbate am I no longer a virgin?
Only sexual intercourse will cause you to no longer be a virgin.

Is masturbation wrong?
Masturbation is not wrong. Even conservative Christian heavyweights such as Dr. James Dobson say masturbation can be a good way to relieve sexual tension. Most teens don't research masturbation before it happens, so they instantly feel guilty for doing it. Doctors say the guilt you feel for masturbating is far more harmful than the act itself. I'll say it again, reader: masturbation is not wrong, and you shouldn't feel guilty about it if you do it. Most teens do it. And most of their parents did it too, whether they want to admit it or not.

Can masturbation be wrong sometimes?
Masturbation is not wrong, but there are some related issues to consider. For instance, if you get addicted to masturbation and use pornography to create the excitement before masturbation, you are entering into some very problematic territory. Because the Internet makes it so easy to access porn, many people get addicted to images and movies of people having sex with each other. Porn addiction is an enormous problem for

many people—men, in particular, and some women too. If you are masturbating regularly by using porn, chances are you are headed for dangerous waters, my friend.

Another thing you have to realize is that the sexual release of masturbation is not the same as the real sex you will have when you are married. Sex is not just a physical act. It is shared by two people who love, trust, and respect one another, and who want to show that love to each other when they make love. If you condition yourself into thinking love-making is just a physical act, your future relationships will suffer. Guys are traditionally guilty of seeing sex as a physical act only. Sex is *way* more— you'll find this out when you fall in love with and marry your soul mate and best friend.

As I said, the Bible really doesn't talk about masturbation. So it doesn't tell us whether or not masturbation is wrong. Of course, it also doesn't tell us Sunday morning golf is wrong, or overindulging in chocolate, or playing the slots, or driving gas-guzzling Hummers. But Scripture does give us guidelines to live by. "'I have the right to do anything'" says 1 Corinthians 6:12, "but not everything is beneficial. 'I have the right to do anything'—but I will not be mastered by anything." So masturbation may never be master over you. You should strive to be master of your own domain. Easier said than done, I know, when you can't get your mind off the latest bump-and-grind music video, but the Bible calls us to be our own masters, to be accountable for our own desires and urges.

So, to recap. You're not going to injure yourself when you masturbate. Most teens do it; many adults do too. You're normal if you do. You shouldn't feel guilty if you do. But you have to be very careful that masturbation isn't the end result of an increasingly lustful appetite. When Graham crackers and Corn Flakes don't work and masturbation becomes intertwined with an addiction to pornography, then you need to talk to someone about strategies to help you be accountable for your actions. Which brings me to the next issue: pornography.

CHAPTER 5

Pornography

First a song . . . with apologies to PINK.

> Dear Mr. Pornographer
> Come take a walk with me.
> Let's pretend we're just neighbors
> Every day my kids you see.
> What do you feel when you know there are children
> logging on?
>
> Who do you pray to when you go to sleep at night
> knowing teens are watching sex?
> What do you feel when you look in the mirror?
> Are you proud?
>
> How do you sleep when the girls who are desperate come
> to you for work?
> How do you dream when a mother has no chance to sav
> her son?
> How do you hold your head up when sex is sapped of love?
> How do you sleep when the whole world is under the
> spell of Internet porn?

I know, it's kind of lame. And out-of-date. It's inspired by a song written a number of years ago by the musical group PINK called "Mr. President" to challenge the American leader on some of his decisions and policies.

The truth is, the world is full of pornographers trying to get your attention. They don't care about you. They don't care about your future boyfriend or girlfriend, your little brother, or your parents either. Pornographers want to show you pictures and videos of naked people having all kinds of sex so that you become addicted and keep coming back. Once pornographers know you are hooked, they smile a big smile. They make billions of dollars off you. And they know that until you get help, you will keep logging on to score your next great feeling.

In the old days, porn came in the form of magazines you could buy at a corner store and videos you could rent from the local video store. You actually had to get into your car or jump on your bike—and try to walk out of the store without bumping into your pastor's wife renting *Mary Poppins.* These days, porn streams right into your house by way of your computer and television. If old-school porn was an addictive drug to your parents' generation, the Internet is the crack cocaine equivalent to your generation. A quick search can score high-def pictures of men and women engaging in sexual acts.

This chapter might be especially difficult for you to read. Maybe the topic hits too close to home. Maybe reading about how God views pornography makes you feel guilty. If so, your first thought might be to close this book and put it back on the shelf. Hey, reader, come take a walk with me. You're not alone. There are lots of teens like you who are struggling with an attraction to pornography. But as you work through this chapter, you'll find out that porn is far from what God intends sex to be. It's sexual entertainment with which to masturbate. And it's wrong.

Perhaps you have only looked at porn a few times. Maybe you're addicted and can't let a week go by without searching for sex sites or downloading videos. If you've never viewed porn or have never stumbled across it, then you are an exception in the world of teens.

But be on your guard! You'll be invited and enticed by e-mails and instant messages from "friends" sending you stuff. You'll be looking for a soccer clip on YouTube and find a list of suggested "soccer mom" videos. You'll be helping your little brother do research for a project on Canada's national animal, the beaver, and find lists of websites that aren't about the buck-toothed little rodent. It's inevitable. And once you go down that alley, it's difficult not to revisit it over and over to recapture the feeling you got. Yep, sounds like drugs alright.

Our culture has become addicted to porn. Did you know that 25 percent of all Internet searches are porn-related (www.healthymind.com)? According to the *New York Times*, half of all hotel guests order pornographic movies and watch them on average for seventeen minutes. Do you know why they only watch for seventeen minutes? That's the time it takes for them to become horny and masturbate. And a Focus on the Family poll found that almost 50 percent of families say pornography is a problem in their homes.

Is porn a problem in your life? You can answer that question silently. Do you deliberately sit down to look for porn on the Internet at least once a week? Have you been tempted to buy a pornographic magazine, or do you find it hard to walk past a magazine rack without looking at the top row to see if you can glimpse anything? If so, you may be a porn addict. Have you ever made promises to yourself and God after you masturbated that you will never look at porn again, only to be lured back to it a few days later?

If you answered yes to any of those questions, you are not alone. Porn addiction is becoming a huge problem for people, particularly males. (If you're a girl, don't get all hoity-toity about your resistance to porn. Stats show that girls and women are increasingly viewing and becoming addicted to porn. While porn doesn't seem to have the same glitter for girls as it does for guys, lots of girls check it out. If your boyfriend wants you to look at porn with him to enhance your feelings toward him, you are entering very dangerous territory and need to reassess your relationship.)

Here's how it works. Pornography is created to cause deep feelings of lust in you (it's called making you feel horny) so that you masturbate. It's as simple as that. There is no mystery or romance in a porn clip. A woman presents herself as sexually available and has sex with one, two, or even three guys until they all have an orgasm. There isn't a more predictable plot line than that of a porn movie; yet those who are addicted will come back to the same pictures and videos over and over again. It's a cycle many people long to free themselves from—but can't.

Let me make this simple and to the point. Viewing porn is *not* part of the healthy sexuality that God designed for us. Sex is meant to be a private, intimate act between husband and wife. God does not want you looking at a naked woman or man and getting horny. I know it sounds blunt, but there's no other way to conk you over the head than with a sentence-hammer (and by using the word *horny*).

In the last chapter, I said that the Bible never mentions masturbation. While God didn't say anything about touching yourself in that way, God does have plenty to say about your viewing of and participation in sex. Listen to what Jesus says in Matthew 5:28-29: "But I tell you that anyone who looks at a woman lustfully has already committed adultery with her in his heart. If your right eye causes you to stumble, gouge it out and throw it away. It is better for you to lose one part of your body than for your whole body to be thrown into hell."

I know—that sounds harsh. But don't think for a minute that Jesus is kidding. He wants you to be respectful of women and men. If you have a boyfriend or girlfriend, that's the person who deserves all your love and attention. And if you don't, porn still represents a fantasy world of unrealistic sex. You are conditioning yourself to see porn as normal sex. And it's not! Check out what Ephesians 5:3 has to say about your sexual interests: "Among you there must not be even a hint of sexual immorality, or of any kind of impurity, or of greed, because these are improper for the Lord's people." Can it be any clearer, my friend?

Look at it this way: God wants you to think pure thoughts. Pornography breeds dirty thoughts. You will long remember the images you see in porn, and eventually you will be hard-wired with attitudes and emotions about sex that have nothing to do with sex between two people who love and care for each other.

Guys, listen up! Porn trains you to think of women as objects on which to project yourself. That's wrong, and there's no place for it in a relationship. If you view porn, you'll find it affecting your relationship—and future relationships. If you introduce your girlfriend to pornography and try to embed it in your relationship, your relationship is on shaky ground—kind of like building it on sand. Porn is quicksand.

Girls, porn trains you to think that your value lies in how well you can satisfy a guy. That's what women do in porn movies. When a husband and wife make love in a trusting, loving marriage, there's no power of one person over the other; there's no dirtiness to sex. If your boyfriend loves and respects you, he will not try to bring other men and women having sex on a screen or in pictures into your relationship. It's as simple as that.

Philippians 4:6-8 says, "Do not be anxious about anything, but in every situation, by prayer and petition, with thanksgiving, present your requests to God. And the peace of God, which transcends all understanding, will guard your hearts and your minds in Christ Jesus. Finally, brothers and sisters, whatever is true, whatever is noble, whatever is right, whatever is pure, whatever is lovely, whatever is admirable—if anything is excellent or praiseworthy—think about such things."

Here's a quiz. I will answer in as many languages as I can.

     Is porn **noble**? *No.*
     Is porn **right**? *Non.*
     Is porn **pure**? *Nein.*
     Is porn **lovely**? *Ney.*
     Is porn **admirable**? *No way, Jose.*

Does porn fit into a healthy relationship between a boyfriend and girlfriend? I think you get the point. There is *no* justification for watching pornography. It hurts you, it hurts your relationships, and it is not part of God's expectations for a healthy sexuality rooted in honesty, respect, and love.

If you are addicted to porn, or if you think you might be, pray the prayer of Psalm 119:35-37: "Direct me in the path of your commands, for there I find delight. Turn my heart toward your statutes and not toward selfish gain. Turn my eyes away from worthless things; preserve my life according to your word." Or use the words of this prayer: "Lord, I am addicted to porn. Please help me stop. And if I can't stop, please give me the courage to tell someone about my problem. I want to be free of my obsession with looking for porn on the Internet. Porn is eating away inside me. It never satisfies me. I need help. I lay my porn addiction at the foot of your cross. Lord, please take it away from me. Amen."

God knows your struggles already. You're not informing him of your difficulty and attraction to porn. But he wants to hear from you about it. Admitting you have a problem is the first step. God will help you get through it if you're willing to listen to his desires for you to be his pure and holy child. Is your sin too big for God to handle? Believe me, he's listening to the prayers of murderers, thieves, and abusers. He can handle your struggles with pornography.

God bless, my friend. I know this wasn't an easy chapter to read. It wasn't an easy one to write, either, because you invited me into your house, and I had to say some tough things to you. I'll leave with you with a Bible passage that helps me when I'm struggling in life. It's Psalm 116:1-8:

> I love the LORD, for he heard my voice;
> he heard my cry for mercy.
> Because he turned his ear to me,
> I will call on him as long as I live.
> The cords of death entangled me,
> the anguish of the grave came over me;
> I was overcome by distress and sorrow.
> Then I called on the name of the LORD:
> "LORD, save me!"
> The LORD is gracious and righteous;
> our God is full of compassion.
> The LORD protects the unwary;
> when I was brought low, he saved me.
> Return to your rest, my soul,
> for the LORD has been good to you.
> For you, LORD, have delivered me from death,
> my eyes from tears,
> my feet from stumbling.

I know, I know, you're not exactly facing death. But sometimes when you struggle with extreme guilt and you're addicted to stuff you long to be free from, it feels like you are dying—on the inside at least. Remember that God's grace has no bounds. He forgives you. He heals you. You are God's child, and he will never abandon you no matter how far into this you are.

CHAPTER 6

Abuse

Hey, reader. Welcome back. We've got another heavy-duty topic to tackle before we get to the chapters about boyfriend/girlfriend relationships. But stick around. The wait will be worth it—almost as worth it as the time you stood in line enduring 103-degree temperature to ride the Dueling Dragon last summer. OK, that was me but, trust me, that ride was worth the wait!

This chapter is about sexual abuse, one of the ugliest, scariest things that can happen to a person. I want to talk to you about this because you or your present/future significant other may have been affected by abuse in some way in the past. Perhaps you wrote about it on your Sex and Relationship Timeline back in chapter 2. Or maybe you know of someone who was sexually abused.

Let's back up a bit. Remember back in the Garden of Eden when God created Adam and Eve and gave them the gift of sexuality? The two of them trusted, loved, and respected each other, and they enjoyed God's gift of sex together. But then that snake, Satan, slithered into the garden and uttered the first lie to a human. "Go ahead and eat the apple, Eve," hissed Satan. "It will feel good." This lie would be repeated over and over again in many different contexts. "It's OK to do this. I won't tell anyone. Trust me."

And so sin entered the world with all the shadiness of a predator. Everything that was once completely beautiful could now be taken and bent out of shape, warped, and stained. While once sex had been perfect and pure, now it had the potential to become evil and dirty in the hands of sinners.

Child porn, sexual abuse, and rape entered the world. In a sense, Satan committed the first rape on humanity. He slid into the life of an innocent woman, told her lies, and enticed her to do things with promises that were fool's gold. The good news is that despite the darkness that descended on earth that very day, there is healing through Jesus Christ. Jesus redeemed our entire sinful, abused world.

The same can be said of anyone affected by sexual abuse. God has the power to heal *you*. No matter how deep your ache, no matter how much you feel no one will believe you, no matter how much you worry that people might blame you. You have to trust me on that. Listen to what David says in Psalm 40:1-2: "I waited patiently for the LORD; he turned to me and heard my cry. He lifted me out of the slimy pit, out of the mud and mire; he set my feet on a rock and gave me a firm place to stand." A couple of verses later, he says, "Many, LORD my God, are the wonders you have done, the things you planned for us." God knows your pain. The evil that happened to you was Satan's doing. God can make it better.

I'm going to tell you straight up—I have never been sexually abused. Aside from the guy who exposed himself to my brother and me when we were kids, I've never fallen prey to a sexual predator. But the reality is that many boys and girls have been molested, touched inappropriately, or used as objects of sexual desire by adults who used their power to abuse defenseless children. If you have been (or are) one of those kids, there's one thing you need to know for sure: *What happened to you was horrible, but no matter what your head is telling you, what happened is not your fault.* The person who touched you and lied to you and threatened you is to blame 100 percent—even if that person is a teacher or a parent or someone at church.

Girls, you are three times more likely to be the victim of sexual abuse than guys. Because our media culture celebrates the female body as an object to be used for pleasure, and because we live in a depraved world, you are in danger of being victimized at any time in your life. If you feel uncomfortable in any situation, trust your instincts and remove yourself from the situation immediately if you can. If something has already happened to you, tell someone you trust about it. As difficult as it may seem, *never* keep what happened to you a secret, even if you have been threatened by your abuser. Tell someone! It's critical to stop what's happening as soon as you can.

Here is one girl's story of abuse:

> When Melanie was twelve years old, her cousins came over for a big Thanksgiving dinner. She wanted to look cool so she put on a bit of eyeliner and a touch of lipstick. Nothing too obvious. Her dad didn't like a lot of make-up on her or her sisters. As they did every Thanksgiving, the guys drank beer and watched football; the girls played games, laughed, and ate plenty of food.
>
> Later in the evening—right before the big feast—Melanie went up to her room to get away from all the noise and to read for a while. A few minutes later, her uncle came into her room and sat on the edge of the bed. He was all smiles, taking an interest in her book and the posters on her walls, asking about her friends and school and lousy teachers.
>
> He moved closer and closer beside her on the bed. Then he grabbed her breast. She let out a squeal but he put his hand over her mouth. He told her that if she said anything to anyone, he would tell her father she'd asked him to come into her bedroom. Melanie was scared. Her uncle left soon after, but she was unable to come down for Thanksgiving dinner. She told her mother she didn't feel well.
>
> Gradually Melanie convinced herself the whole thing was just something she had dreamed about. Two months later, her parents asked her uncle to pick her up from school because they were both working late. Melanie told her mother she didn't want a ride from Uncle Marty, but she refused to give an answer when her mother asked her why. Her mother told her to quit acting like a brat. On the way home, her uncle touched her again, but this time he went further, exposing himself to her. He also gave her a digital music player and told her no one needed to know anything. It would be their secret, he said, and he had lots of other cool stuff for her.
>
> The abuse went on until Melanie was sixteen and got her first boyfriend. Then her uncle stopped. Melanie worried

about her little sister. But she tried to forget about her problems by spending lots of time with her new boyfriend. They had only been going out three weeks before Melanie initiated sex with him.

At home she couldn't look at herself in the mirror because she thought she was ugly and worthless. There were mornings she didn't get out of bed to go to school. Once she missed six straight days of school. Her parents blamed her erratic behavior on her new boyfriend. Melanie was disgusted with herself, but she couldn't help wanting to have sex with her boyfriend whenever they were alone.

Some days Melanie thinks it would be better to just kill herself. She doesn't know where to turn. . . .

There are many stories like Melanie's, of course, but the theme is always the same. Someone forces another person to do something he or she doesn't want to do. The effects of that abuse ripples out and touches many people, but it hurts the abused person most of all. A person who is abused as a child or teen will be fearful and cautious about relationships from then on.

Maybe you "get that" in a way no one will ever, ever know.

When trust in a relationship is broken, it can affect all of your relationships in a big way *until you get help*. Melanie, the girl who was abused by her uncle, walked this journey of abuse alone. She couldn't even look at school pictures taken during those years because she hated the Melanie in those pictures. She blamed *that* Melanie for what happened to her—almost as if *that* Melanie were a different person. So she ripped down every poster, every piece of artwork from those years.

Her parents couldn't understand why Melanie had changed so much. They said things like, "What happened to the old Melanie who used to come home from school and couldn't stop talking?" or "Where is that little girl who used to spend hours writing stories in her journal?" Melanie knew her old self was dead, murdered by the uncle who'd stolen her innocence. Over time, Melanie began to believe people were disgusted with her, even though they didn't know what had happened—as if it were somehow her fault.

Let me point out here that girls *and* boys are the victims of abuse, just as men *and* women can be abusers. The reality, however, is that the majority of sexual abusers are men and the majority of children who are sexually abused are girls. You will probably never know who has been abused because most of them will keep it a dark secret.

Here's what can happen to you if you've been sexually abused as a child and later begin a relationship with someone of the opposite sex:

- You might hate your own body because of what happened to you. You might feel as if your body has betrayed you. Perhaps you struggle with an eating disorder. When you hate yourself—outside and inside—you will have a difficult time loving anyone else.
- You may have a hard time trusting people, including your boyfriend or girlfriend. You might flinch at his or her touch or find yourself rigid during those moments you are alone.
- You might not be able to be physically close with your boyfriend or girlfriend, or, later on, with your husband or wife. When you are close, you undermine the moment by breaking away or laughing. This is your unconscious reaction in order to avoid situations that once brought you pain. If you feel fear and shame about a past experience, it is sometimes difficult for you to move forward with someone you like a lot—or even love.
- Like Melanie, you may become hyper-sexual with your boyfriend or girlfriend. People who were abused may respond by acting out in the very way they were abused. For boys, this means imitating the abuser and exerting wrongful power over their girlfriends or others. For girls, it most often means playing the role of victim; or in some cases playing the role of sexual aggressor because that's the role that led to "acceptance."
- You may feel anxious and depressed. Your self-esteem has taken a beating at the hands of someone who has made you feel guilty and maybe even threatened you to keep quiet.
- You may feel like you'd like to die. Sadly, that's a common feeling for many abused kids.

If you've been abused or violated in any way; if you recognize yourself in these descriptions, I repeat: get help. Talk to someone you trust who will listen to you, respect you, and put you in touch with the professional help you need. That person might be a family friend or your best friend's parents. Or you can call a toll-free abuse hotline; you'll find the number in your phone book. You need to know you are not alone—many others are also victims of sexual abuse.

It's hard to imagine why Melanie's uncle could do those terrible things to his own niece, isn't it? The reality is that in most cases, the person who is abused knows the abuser—and all too often the abuser is a member of the family, which makes telling someone else about it very difficult. Why do people abuse others sexually? It's *not* about the sex. An abuser is motivated by the power and control it gives him over another person. Usually an abuser looks to control and dominate people who are younger, weaker, and more vulnerable.

The destruction and damage caused by abuse can never be undone. But the good news is that healing can take place. That's why if someone has abused you in any way, you really need to tell someone you trust—and you need to do it *now*. If it's easier, write it all down and give it to that person you trust. He or she will hook you up with a professional counselor who understands what you've been through and who is able to help you heal. With that help and the support of loved ones, you can begin to rebuild your self-esteem. You can learn to love yourself and your body again. And in the healing process, you'll learn that sexual intimacy is a wonderful gift from God—a gift for you from the Creator who loves you!

If this chapter shot an arrow right at your heart, dear reader, please know that I'm praying for you. Remember that God loves you, no matter what happened to you. And God's power is able to overpower the evil that slithered into your own personal garden.

CHAPTER 7

The Tingle!

Every Sunday night, my wife used to grab a box of Kleenex and make me watch the TV show *Extreme Makeover: Home Edition* with Ty Pennington, the coolest interior designer/carpenter you've ever seen. A group of interior designers and carpenters connects with a family that has gone through some kind of personal tragedy. They usually send the family to Disneyland while they build a new house for them. Did I watch the show because I like to see rooms get painted and new kitchens get installed? (Does an Emperor penguin like standing in minus-100-degree weather with an egg on top of his feet while his mate goes to get food from the ocean?) No, but for the good of my marriage I watched, just like my wife sometimes watches *Monday Night Football* with me. It draws us closer.

Guys, you learn quickly that when you go to chick flicks with your girlfriend, listen with interest to her difficulties with her friends, and help her pick out new earrings at the mall on Saturday morning, you are earning major brownie points.

Girls, your man will look at you and smile a lot more when you tell him he looks great in his new jeans or that he played well in the chess tournament after school yesterday.

The good news is, you'll have no problem doing these things in the weeks leading up to your "going out" and during the first three months after you start going out. (We'll get to that in chapter 8, "Those First Three Months." And we'll get to the post-honeymoon stage of your relationship in chapter 9, "When Cracks Appear"—and I'm not talking about going to a plasterers' convention.)

You see, relationships—including girlfriend-boyfriend relationships—follow a certain pattern. If you've already had a long-term relationship with a girl or guy, you will know what I mean. So this chapter is for your *next* romantic endeavor (don't tell your current boyfriend/girlfriend I said that!). And if you've never had a girlfriend or boyfriend, this chapter aims to prepare you for what often happens in those glorious moments after you catch each other's gaze and realize someone likes you—and you get that tingle.

Once again, I'll take out the pickle jar to answer some oft-asked questions about what is acceptable and what is not during the "pre" stages of the relationship.

I started this chapter with a reference to the TV show *Extreme Makeover: Home Edition*. If you've ever watched it, you'll know the show doesn't jump right in with opening credits, followed immediately by carpenters swinging hammers and framing the new house. Instead the story builds slowly. First, the *Makeover* crew discovers a needy family, next they assess whether they want to get involved, then they figure out the work that needs to be done—and *then* they dive into the project.

While I'd hate to imply that having a girlfriend or boyfriend is like *Extreme Makeover*, the pattern in the early stages is kind of similar. (Plus my wife likes it when I talk about Ty Pennington—man, I want to be like that guy.)

What happens is you'll wake up one day (it might be during math class) and realize that the person two rows over is always laughing at your jokes or showing up in the hallway of your school right where you happen to be. But you won't be sure he or she actually likes you, so you definitely don't walk over and ask the person out like you might in a sitcom. You quietly feel good about yourself for a while and enjoy the attention.

If you like the person back, you will begin laughing at his or her jokes and agreeing to join whatever group he or she's a part of during lunch when everyone walks to Micky D's for burgers. You might also start doing things you've never done before to let that person know you have feelings for him or her—things like skipping class or challenging a teacher publicly who disagrees with your new potential flame's answer about the American Revolution.

All these things will help send the message that you've awakened to the possibility that this person likes you, and the feeling is mutual. You'll also keep an out to make sure this person doesn't act this way with *everyone*. So, for instance, if this person who wants to be your partner in gym class for square dancing picks someone else to solve a Sudoku in accounting class, you just might lose your confidence. Then it's OK to sit back and assess your potential flame.

OK, first pickle jar question:

Is there really such a thing as love at first sight?
I believe *infatuation* at first sight is probably the more appropriate word for that sentence. The reality is you will be smitten with the way a person looks, how she turns around and laughs, the way she looks when she walks down the hall, the very cute way she straightens her hair, how heavenly she smells. You will tingle when you see him smile, look at the hair on the back of his hand, glimpse his shoulder blades through his T-shirt, soak in his sense of humor.

But you don't actually know this person. If you've been in a relationship before, you'll know that sometimes, six months down the road, you feel duped—big time—about what you thought she was like. On the other hand, maybe you will have caught a glimpse of heaven during those initial meetings and love your flame even deeper after six months because you know him so much better than when you first started staring at him.

Is it OK to ask someone out by e-mail or instant messaging?
I never had a chance to text someone to see if they wanted to go to a movie, but your generation of friends is attached at the fingertips. I would say it's OK if you know the person. The nicest thing about personal web pages and IM is that a whole group of you can plan a night out. That's a non-threatening way for you to spend time with your potential girl or guy friend. Also keep in mind that nothing's more awkward than asking someone to the fall fair and watching them ponder for seven seconds before saying they have to bathe their dog that night. In that case, e-mail or texting might be a safe way to avoid some embarrassment!

Is it OK for a girl to ask a guy out?
Girls and women want equality in all areas of life, but strangely we have some traditional views of guy-girl interactions. One is that guys should

be the ones asking girls out. Let me tell you something: I'd probably be single and celibate right now if the girls in my life didn't take charge of me. I could never get past the stage of "Does she *really* like me?" (Remember my third-grade experience with Jodie Ann?)

Girls, it is totally, 100 percent acceptable for you to ask a guy to get ice cream or to see *Spiderman 16*. It's also mucho-acceptable for you to ask a guy to be your boyfriend. If the guy has a problem with this, see it as a warning sign and start swimming around that great big sea for another fish, sister!

Should I only go on group dates first?
Going on group "dates" is a great way to get to know a person in a non-threatening way. You can observe the person you like as you figure out whether a solo flight is in the crystal ball. Eventually, to get to the next phase of a relationship, you will want to be alone with your friend, but you can do this in a non-threatening way too. Go to movies, go bowling, go to a basketball game, go to the mall. The bottom line is to have fun together. You don't want to get all caught up in intimate complexities right from the start, no matter what that choir of hormones is singing to you. Work on honesty, good communication, and respect for each other—that's the best way to build a strong relationship.

What actually happens so we know we are going steady?
Usually, after going on group dates and then going out together on single dates, you find yourself still interested in taking your new close friend's calls and texts. The traditional way would be for the guy to say, "Will you go with me?" The girl would answer yes and *voila!*—you're a couple. You might now hold hands in public and maybe kiss each other goodbye at the end of dates. These will be signals to others that both of you are now off-limits to others. I once liked a girl a lot, but never got to the stage of asking her to go with me. My older brother, of all people, moved in on her and asked her out!

Sometimes guys and girls feel like they are *kind of* going out, but they've never actually gone through the formal steps of communicating this fact to one another. They just start holding hands; they just start being alone together and everyone just . . . knows. My advice if you find yourself in a situation like this? One of you needs to initiate a conversation that goes something like this: "Where are we at?" It may not be the best grammar, but it could be one of the most important questions you ask—not only because the two of you will answer the question together, but you will start your relationship on solid ground by communicating openly with each other. More about that later.

OK, so you've noticed each other's best features, you've gone bowling and to youth group beach day, you've gone to see the latest chick flick at the Cineplex, and you've gazed into one another's eyes and confessed you would really like to go out. That cheering you hear is your choir of hormones exploding into the "Hallelujah Chorus." You are now holding hands. Everyone knows you are an item. You are now *Ron and Karen* and not just *Ron*.

You wake up every morning knowing that despite the uncertainty of English essays and quizzes on the periodic table of the elements, there is a constant in your life. Your new boyfriend. Your new girlfriend. Life is good. You thank God every night before you go to bed for bringing this wonderful person into your life. If you are at this stage of your relationship, my brother or sister, you'll be on cruise control for about three months. Love is gloriously blind. You will not, and I repeat, *will not* notice anything remotely bad about your new best friend of the opposite sex. Enjoy it to the fullest!

CHAPTER 8
Those First Three Months

Remember how, in the Introduction to this book, I speculated about Adam and Eve's relationship before the two of them fell into sin? Laughing and giggling together. Going for walks, holding hands, slow dancing under the stars. That's what the first three months of your new relationship will be like.

Even your parents will be interesting to you for a while because all is well in the world. That 57 percent you got on the history quiz? Who cares! Coach told you to get your head in the game after going one for seven from the line last night? No big deal! You are seeing all of life with heightened clarity. The birds sound sweeter. The TV news seems to be getting better. You might even be willing to consider asking your siblings questions about *their* lives.

Shakespeare coined the phrase "love is blind" in his play *The Merchant of Venice*. What he meant, of course, is that when you fall in love with someone, you tend not to see anything even remotely close to reality. Not only will the world around you seem perfect, your new boyfriend or girlfriend will be the center of your universe.

That feeling is awesome. You won't feel jealous. You will accept every excuse and apology. It is one of the times your love—like God's love for you—will be totally unconditional. You not only don't see the warts, you refuse to believe this person could possibly have any. And by warts, you know I don't mean those ugly little hard things on your knuckles. We're talking about all those little things that might bug you in about . . . three months. How she doesn't listen that closely to you while you tell her about the game. How he never seems to want you to hang around with your friends. That stuff. You won't even start asking those questions until about three months. But that's a discussion for the next chapter.

What I'd like to do in this chapter is interview a couple who have been through a boyfriend/girlfriend relationship and seen the pattern. They once were blind but now they see. Let me introduce you to Laura and James—and let them tell you what they learned.

Me: Thanks for coming in to my book today to talk to us about what you learned during your time as a couple. Let me start by asking how long the two of you have been going out.

Laura: A year.

Me: Wow, congratulations. I've been talking to readers about the first three months after a girl and guy start going out—that wonderful time when everything seems *perfect*. What advice would the two of you give to guys and girls out there who are just starting out in a relationship?

James: Stop before it's too late! Just kidding, Ron. Before I start, I just want to give all the glory to God for my relationship and for bringing Laura into my life. Thanks, I've always wanted to do that—like those guys who get interviewed right after the Super Bowl.

If you're just starting out, I'd say be very careful about blocking out the friends you had before you started going out. I had a buddy named Doug who actually had a role in hooking me and Laura up. Once we started going out, I didn't have time for Doug anymore. He always said he understood, but I regret that I didn't balance my time better between Laura and Doug.

Laura: I agree! My friends got really mad at me and stopped talking to me for a while because I like totally ditched them when I started going out with James. Now I can't believe I did that and we're all cool again, but for a while there I wanted to walk home with James every single day after school.

Now when I think back on it I feel terrible. I even stopped going to movies and having sleepovers with my girlfriends. The crazy thing is, I've been on the other side of that—watching my friends hook up with guys and do nothing but hang out with them or talk on the computer with them.

James: I have to admit I didn't like it when she went out with her friends. I don't know . . . I kind of thought I'd lose her if she got back to normal again with them. Like she'd see another guy or something if I wasn't around her every minute. We're still struggling with that even after a whole year. I get jealous when she goes off and does things without me.

Me: What do you do now in your relationship that you didn't do then?

Laura: We're more honest with each other now. When we started getting honest with each other it was hard. We had a lot of fights and almost broke up. But then we started really listening and trusting each other.

James: I'm not real great at talking about our relationship, but I have to agree with Laura. Once we started actually talking about stuff and trusting that the other person wasn't going to laugh or take off or something when one of us had a concern, our relationship got a lot better. And guys, *do not* try to have a conversation with your girlfriend while you're watching the Pistons-Bulls game. I can tell you it does not work.

Me: Do you guys pray together?

Laura: (*she looks at James and they share a smile*) Funny you should mention that. About two-and-a-half months ago, we had a great big fight. James lied to me about what he was doing one night, and then I accused him of cheating on me even though I had no proof. We were making accusations about each other and saying things just to be mean. I was crying and we just sat there in his parents' minivan, not knowing what to do or say next.

James: It was all Laura's idea. She saved us. She turned to me and actually reached over to hold my hand. I thought she wanted to make out—that's how stupid I was. But this was all new territory for me. Laura asked me if I would pray with her about us. I just said yes. And then she started to pray, thanking God for me and for our relationship and asking God to please help us right now. We both started bawling.

You're not going to sell this book at my school I hope, 'cause my friends are going to give me major-league grief if they get their hands on it. Anyway, that was the turning point in our relationship, and now we still pray together.

Me: Is there anything else you would like to share about what to expect in a couple of months?

James: Guys, you are going to wake up one day and start caring about sports, school, and your friends again. You'll have to work hard the *other way* not to leave your girlfriend out of things. She might not be as amazing to you as you thought she was a couple of months ago.

But like Ron says, you weren't seeing things realistically then. She still *is* amazing, but in a more real way. You're going to see her when she's sick and when she has her period. You're going to watch her flip out about her parents. You're going to have to figure out a way to balance your relationship with her and all those other things you care about.

Laura: Girls, you have to remember it's not all about you. The guy may have chased you and done all the work to get you together, but you have to give back too. Guys like attention too. And guys are a little more jealous than girls are—pretty soon your boyfriend might show signs he's mad at you because of the attention you are showing to other friends.

All I can say is, the two of you have to talk about this stuff in an open way, and girls, keep your eyes open to how your boyfriend is responding to you.

Me: I'd like to thank the two of you for appearing in my book today. I wish you both well in your relationship. God bless.

Laura and James: Thanks, Ron. Our pleasure.

So that was Laura and James. Now let's end this chapter with a couple of pickle jar questions.

How far should a boyfriend and girlfriend go during that first three months? You, of course, are talking about how far physically you should go. I think it's reasonable to expect you will probably hold hands, have your arms around each other a lot, and do plenty of "making out." As for touching other body parts . . . that is a very difficult question to answer. I'd say you should spend the majority of your relationship in the first three months talking to each other and getting to know one another. Hold off on touching body parts and exploring territory that your choir of hormones keeps singing about.

Here's something you should know: no matter how far you go, *that* will be the starting point next time. It is very difficult to go backwards to a previous phase in terms of how far you went. Lay down the foundation of your relationship in the early months—that foundation is 95 percent *communication*. And remember that *everything* you do should be governed by trust, respect, and love for the other person. If you venture outside of these basic boundaries God sets for you in all of your relationships, you surely won't be taking good care of the gift God has given you.

What if I'm always the one to make the first move to hold hands or kiss? Should I be concerned?

This is a big one for guys. It says a lot about who is controlling the relationship.

Girls, guys actually care about stuff like this. If you never make the move to hold his hand, he will try to interpret things. What if she doesn't like me anymore? Is she not holding my hand now because she likes that guy over there and wants to appear to be available? Guys are weird when it comes to this stuff.

My advice, as always, is to talk about these things. Ask questions! "Do you like it when I hold your hand across the aisle in math class?" Then be prepared for a realistic answer. If she answers yes but really means no because she is afraid of how you will react, you've got problems, brother. Girls, maybe your boyfriend *hates* it when you're all over him when you meet at his locker. Accept each other's answers. Talk honestly with one another, and start building your relationship on a foundation of truth and trust.

Well, congrats on making it through the blissfully blind period of your relationship. You have now arrived at the gates of chapter 9: "When Cracks Appear."

But first . . . a message from a sponsor.

You know how you watch a YouTube video and a commercial comes on before you get to the video? Kind of annoying, right? It's a really clever way for Coke or Nike to sell their message while you're sitting there tapping your foot impatiently with your hand on the mouse trying to move the little needle on your video player ahead to bypass the commercial (but you can't because the whole video hasn't downloaded yet). You'd never expect a writer guy to use that technique, would you?

Cue Announcer's deep, resonant voice:

Before we get to the chapter on cracks, here is an ad from one of our sponsors for . . . singleness.

Picture two girls standing in front of a camera—like those Mac and PC commercials from a few years back. (If you haven't seen the commercials, put down the book and look them up on YouTube so you know where this is going.) The girls in this YouTube video look the same. They're wearing the same clothes every girl walking to classes in your high school is wearing, their hair is the same style as most of the girls in your English class. But these girls are different. Cue the Mac and PC piano music. . . .

Free Agent: Hi, I'm a free agent.

Girlfriend:: And I'm a girlfriend.

Free Agent: Hey, girlfriend, watcha doing?

Girlfriend: Oh, I'm just getting ready to go out with my boyfriend.

Free Agent: Oh, you have another boyfriend?

Girlfriend: Yeah, for six months now. And what are *you* doing?

Free Agent: I'm going out with some friends.

Girlfriend: You mean *girl*friends, right?

Free Agent: No, actually, two guys and three girls are going out tonight.

Girlfriend: Oh, I get it. You probably want to go out with one of the guys, right? That's why you invited them.

Free Agent: No, actually, we're just friends and we're going to a movie and the Mocha Café afterwards.

Girlfriend: Oh, they're probably ugly, right?

Free Agent: Actually, both guys are really hot.

Girlfriend: Then why aren't you going after one of them?

Free Agent: I'm not ready for a boyfriend yet. Not everyone needs a boyfriend, you know.

Girlfriend: I don't *need* a boyfriend. I just *have* this really awesome boyfriend.

Free Agent: That's great, girlfriend. You two seem really happy together.

Girlfriend: Don't you have any interest in, you know, getting it on?

Free Agent: Of course I do. But the right guy hasn't come along yet and I'm not spending all my waking hours looking for him. I've got too many other things to do.

Girlfriend: But aren't you afraid you'll never get married? I mean, you're going to be eighteen.

Free Agent: Come on, girlfriend. I'm still seventeen. I've got tons of time to get married—if I get married at all. Like I said, the right guy hasn't come along. I like my space and my freedom. Are you going to marry this guy?

Girlfriend: Well, of course I am, free agent.

Free Agent: But didn't you say that about what's his name—

Girlfriend: He didn't work out. I'm learning from each guy.

Free Agent: That's cool. I hope the two of you have a great time tonight. Where are you going?

Girlfriend: I think we're going to a hockey game and then after that we usually go and make out.

Free Agent: Cool.

Girlfriend: Who's all going to Mocha Café?

Free Agent: The regular gang. Whoever shows up. Hey, you should catch up with us later.

Girlfriend: But wouldn't it be awkward. You know, me having a boyfriend and everything and none of you at that stage yet?

Free Agent: Not at all. We're going to see a great movie and have some Ice Caps afterwards. Show up later if you feel like it.

Girlfriend: I'll probably have my hands full, if you know what I mean.

Free Agent: OK, see you around.

Even though the content of this book is geared towards guys and girls who are in teenage relationships with one another, this commercial was for all guys and girls who *don't* have a boyfriend or girlfriend. The myth is you're sitting at home playing checkers with your parents or reading the *Harry Potter* books for the thirteenth time. But of course, you're probably doing whatever you'd like to be doing.

If you're not in a relationship and have no interest in a relationship at this point in your life, kudos, my friend (I've actually never used that word before!). Enjoy your guy and girl friends. Having fun, talking, and learning about the opposite sex is what fills the pie chart of most relationships, and you can learn a lot about that aspect of your relationship with card-carrying members of the opposite sex by going to movies and the cappuccino café on Friday night.

Paul is pretty blunt in 1 Corinthians 7:7 when he shares his feelings about singleness: "I wish that all of you were [single] as I am. But each of you has your own gift from God; one has this gift [of marriage], another has that [of singleness]." Paul's reason for wanting people to be single is so they can spend more time doing God's work and not thinking about how great your boyfriend's pecs look when he plays shirts and skins in three-on-three after school. He's got a point, I suppose.

Now, cue Announcer's voice again:

Coming up . . . When cracks appear in your relationship. . . .

CHAPTER 9

When Cracks Appear

Remember a few pages back when you I told you a typical high school boyfriend/girlfriend relationship follows a predictable pattern? We've covered the pre-relationship phase (when you first discover this person who makes you tingle!) and the first-three-months phase (when the two of you are goofy and blind to each other and to everything around you). The pre-relationship phase often happens around three weeks into the school year, at which point the boyfriend and girlfriend become an official unit. The next phase generally lasts right through Christmas, which is actually the height of this blissful, blinding time.

Guess what happens in January when everyone comes back to school after Christmas break? You guessed it—cracks begin to show in the relationship. Now, this isn't a science. The pattern may play itself out again with new relationships starting up in January, lasting until spring break, then faltering when everyone comes back to school with deep tans and braided hair. The point is, the pattern is predictable whenever it happens, and my job is to let you know what may be coming down the road.

For some of you who have been in longer-term relationships and have gone through the issues I'll address here, this may be a difficult chapter to read. For many of you, this phase was the last phase of your relationship because you discovered things about your partner you didn't like and ended up texting a Dear John or Dear Joanne message. And perhaps some of you went from the Disneyland phase straight into a phase where you gave way too much to your partner and now you feel like there's no turning back.

I wrote this chapter to help you do two things: first, to recognize the challenges and decisions that you can expect; and second, to let your faith guide your response when you're faced with those decisions. Here's what's ahead:

- We are going to talk about those hot-and-heavy moments in your bedroom when your parents are gone for the weekend and he or she won't take no for an answer.
- We are going to talk about dating violence and the difficulty of getting out of a relationship with someone who controls and manipulates you.
- We are going to talk about the importance of communication and the need to prepare yourself for the possibility that one of you might want to have sex—not the feeling-each-other-up-probing-with-your-tongue kind of sex. I mean the drop-your-pants-take-off-your-underwear-intercourse-when-you're-heavy-in-the-moment kind of sex.
- We are going to talk about the idea of signing an abstinence contract with your partner.
- And, you might also be surprised to know, we are going to talk about using condoms.

For this chapter, I am going to click on my "inbox" and reply to guys and girls all across this great land who have entered the gates of serious relationships. I'm guessing you might be shocked by some of the things going on inside these relationships. It's good to know where you're headed before you begin, correct? You wouldn't climb Mount Everest without first talking to or reading about people who have attempted the climb, right?

Consider this chapter your guide to getting to the summit of your relationship. You've probably guessed that the summit might be the day you walk down the aisle together with both families snapping pictures as the two of you stand nervously at the front of the church. But the journey to the summit is not an easy one. You just might decide it's not for you and enjoy the single life for a stretch of time—there's nothing wrong with that. You might attempt the climb several times before finding the right partner for scaling those cliffs and enduring those wicked snowstorms.

Enough already—this metaphor is getting cheesy. The point is that you will probably have several boyfriends or girlfriends with whom you make decisions about many of the issues you'll read about in this chapter. Eventually you may find that special someone with whom you decide to spend your life—ending this part of the journey and beginning a whole new life together. That's when everyone gathers and throws three-hole-punch waste at you. But that place is still up in the clouds somewhere.

OK, here we go. You're through the tingly phase. You're through the three-month, my-partner-can't-do-anything-wrong phase. You've remembered that you still have other friends, you love basketball, and you need to start volunteering again at your church. Your relationship with your boyfriend or girlfriend is now *one* of the things you care about—not the *only* thing you care about.

This is usually the point when you start to fight about some things. You will have questions. Let's look at some of the e-mails I've received from readers like you:

Message:

> My boyfriend and I have been going out for three months. He's great. Up until now, we've had a blast together. All the girls think he's cool. So far we have held hands and made out in the car after a movie or youth group, but now we're finding ourselves going to the next level.
>
> Last week my boyfriend put his hand on my breast and started squeezing it. Then he pulled my shirt out and slid his hand up to my bra. I stopped kissing him and pulled his wrist down. He got really mad and asked me what the big problem was. I told him I didn't want him touching me there. He asked why not. I didn't really have an answer for him, and that made him even madder.
>
> He scared me by driving home really fast after that, and then he didn't call for two days. We didn't talk about it at all and just kinda forgave each other, I guess. Last night we were making out again and he did the same thing. This time I let him because I didn't want a rerun of last time. He told me he really loved me after I let him, and this morning he gave me these cute little earrings.
>
> But I feel sort of guilty about it. Did I do the right thing by letting him touch me there when I told him before he couldn't? —*Confused in Michigan*

Response:

Thanks for writing, Michigan.

Your boyfriend seems ready to go to the next level, but you aren't. Letting him touch your breasts the second time has taught your boyfriend that when he wants something from you, all he has to do is get mad at you and you'll eventually cave in and give him what he wants.

I'm worried for you. Your boyfriend is showing classic signs of control and manipulation. Sex is a gift from God, but it has boundaries, and God has basic expectations for both of you. Your boyfriend broke two fundamental boundaries. He didn't respect you, and he broke your trust.

I think you know this will happen again. Giving you a gift after you gave in is further evidence that he will reward you when you please him and get mad (and put your life in danger by driving fast) when you don't.

What also worries me is that you and your boyfriend didn't talk about what happened the first night. (You said you "kinda forgave each other.") Your boyfriend is playing classic mind games with you. You need to talk openly and honestly about what happened that first night.

Your boyfriend has to understand and respect that when you don't want to do something he wants to do, he *must* stop. He may say things like, "If you really loved me, you wouldn't stop me. Maybe you don't really love me." If this happens, you need to seriously consider talking to someone (a parent or guidance counselor) for advice or help with deciding whether you want to continue this relationship.

If your boyfriend really loves you, he will respect your concerns and try to move forward in your relationship at your pace. You also need to take a stand in your relationship so that when your boyfriend suggests making out, you can take that opportunity to tell him why you are uncomfortable doing that. Again, if he loves and respects you and doesn't want to lose you, he will listen and comply.

What you also have to be worried about is that your boyfriend will not stop at touching your breasts. Soon he will want to go further. You need to talk honestly and sincerely to him about what you are comfortable with and what you are *not* comfortable with. Set your own boundaries and let him know that when he crosses the line, he is not respecting and loving you. And that's just not acceptable. *—Ron*

Message

My girlfriend and I have been going out for about six months now. Everyone says we're pretty much married already because we're inseparable, and we kind of treat each other like a husband and wife. She gets a bit cranky with me and everyone laughs because I take it. It's just the way we are.

She's really good-looking, you know, a real head-turner. And she's not one of those prudes—my girlfriend likes to go at it, if you know what I mean. Usually she does the initiating. When I'm driving, she'll put her hand on my thigh and just start tracing her fingers up my jeans real close like. She knows I'd do just about anything for her when she does that.

Lately, my girlfriend has these times when she kind of shuts me out completely. We share a locker at school, and there are days when she'll slam her books on the shelf, grab her coat, and just leave me standing there by myself. It's kind of embarrassing. Then I have to spend the next day or two figuring out why she's mad at me. It's usually because I wasn't online at ten the night before like we apparently had agreed. Or because I didn't stick up for her when her friend was dissing her in the cafeteria. I never really know when she's going to get mad.

Other times, when she wants something from me, she's all over me. Man, can that woman go at it! During those times I'm in heaven. But every time I try to talk to her about freezing me out she pretends she doesn't have a clue what I'm talking about and tells me I'm being stupid. Is this normal? —*Toronto*

Response:

Your girlfriend is controlling you big time, my brother. She does it in two ways. She shuts you out and keeps you guessing. And she uses sex as a weapon. In both cases, you're on a short leash. I feel your pain. I once had a girlfriend like this. You love the making-out part, but the days when you're walking around wondering what's going on are painful.

I'm impressed that you've tried to talk to her about your feelings. Communication is the key to trust and respect in a relationship. What I'm concerned about, though, is that she tells you you're stupid when you talk openly about your concerns—and she pretends not to know it's going on. Is it possible she truly doesn't realize what she's doing, and this is just her personality? If so, you need to strongly consider whether or not to continue your relationship with her.

A way in which you can exert your own power is by refusing those moments when she is using sex to groom you for things she wants later. When you take away her power, she will become confused and confront you. This may be a gateway to that conversation you've been trying to initiate.

If you can't get anywhere on your own, you might want to talk to someone you trust about it. If your girlfriend truly cares about your relationship, she should agree to talk to someone with you. If she still refuses to communicate or work on the relationship, one of two things is going to happen: you are going to shut up and put up with it or you will break off the relationship. Control and manipulation have no place in a loving friendship between two people who respect and trust each other. —Ron

> Message:
>
> My girlfriend and I have been going out for almost a year. We've got a great relationship and are best friends. We both want to be teachers and are going off to college soon. Do you think it's OK for us to go to separate colleges when we graduate from high school? I'm worried she'll meet someone else and consider our relationship one of those high school flings she had when she was a kid or something. Our colleges are clear across the state from each other and we won't see each other until Christmas. —Scared in California

Response:

I understand your worries. You didn't mention whether or not you talked this over with your girlfriend, but I'll assume you did since you are best friends. Remember, *communication is the number one rule* in a relationship.

You might be worried that your girlfriend will interpret your worries as not trusting her. That's possible, but I doubt she'll respond that way since you said you have a great relationship. The good news is your generation is more connected than any previous generation. You can e-mail each other every day, or even get a webcam and text each other face-to-face. Ah, technology!

You might be surprised by the kinds of things you will "talk about" in e-mail—things you might not have talked about when you saw each other every day. The reality is your relationship will weather the storm of separation if you love each other.

Pray for each other and for your relationship. God will take care of each of you on your separate campuses and he will bring you back together again one day if his will says so. And have a great school year. —*Ron*

> *Message:*
>
> How long should we wait to invite each other over for dinner with each other's families? Also, should I buy an expensive Christmas present for my boyfriend? We've been going out for three whole months. —*Iowa*

Response:

There's no formula for or rule about when you can invite your boyfriend to your house for dinner. What I'd suggest is to ask your parents and also your boyfriend if they are comfortable with the idea. You don't want an awkward situation to go down because your dad hates it that you have a boyfriend, for instance. Also, you want your boyfriend to feel comfortable with the idea of meeting your family.

As silly as it sounds, lots of boyfriends and girlfriends make some big decisions about the relationship after meeting each other's family. If your mother eats with her fingers and has a shotgun across her lap, for instance, your boyfriend might think you'll eventually be like that too.

The question about buying your boyfriend an expensive present is tough to answer. I really don't know what you consider expensive. When I was a senior in high school saving up for college, a CD was expensive for me. If you think the value of a present is going to say something about how you feel about your boyfriend, you're way off base. If you make a card and

write your own poem or note telling him how much you like/love him, if you spend time making something for him, that will mean more than anything you could purchase at Wal-Mart. Save your money for college!
—*Ron*

Message:

When my boyfriend gets really mad at me for being late, he will sometimes push me into the car. One time, when I told him to chill, he reached over and grabbed me by the hair and told me I'd better watch myself. It hurt when he did that, but then a few minutes later he apologized and even cried because he didn't know what had gotten into him. He never really wants to be with my friends and hates them all, especially my guy friends. He sometimes calls them "gay" and says he's going to beat the crap out of them one day. — *Vancouver*

Response:

You are in a relationship that is clearly abusive, and you need to get help today. Talk to an adult you trust—a guidance counselor, pastor, parent, or teacher—and tell that person the truth about what is happening. What your boyfriend is doing is called assault. And not only is it not acceptable in a relationship, he could be charged by the police for what he is doing. No boyfriend has the right to physically hurt his girlfriend (and vice versa, of course).

You said he apologized and even cried after he did it. Maybe you feel sorry for *him* during these moments. Don't! This is classic abuser behavior. It excuses the abuse and paves the way for the next incident when he will flare up and possibly harm you.

What's worse, if you begin to believe this is normal behavior, you will probably do everything you can to pacify him and to prevent his abusive behavior toward you. This means he has 100 percent control over you. You will drop your girlfriends and stop talking to your guy friends simply because you want to keep your boyfriend happy—and to avoid further abusiveness. If you do this, girl, you are headed for a long, unhappy relationship.

Trust me, getting married won't solve this dilemma—it will get even worse. My advice: break up with this guy *now*. Be careful, though, when you leave an abusive partner. Tell other people about it too, and make sure you choose a safe, public place to have that conversation. Even if he is an abuser because he himself was abused, this is not your project to fix. You are not on a rescue mission, and you will not transform him into a gentle, handsome prince. This is not *Beauty and the Beast*. You don't have to feel guilty for abandoning him. This is his problem, and he needs anger management intervention and major-league counseling. I pray you will have the courage to walk away from this abusive situation before it's too late. God bless. —*Ron*

> *Message:*
>
> My girlfriend wants to stay pure until we get married, which means keeping our clothes on and going no further than kissing and hugging. We've been going out for a year-and-a-half now.
>
> Friends of ours—a couple who go to our high school— have what's called cybersex. They get on their computers, turn on their webcams, and take off their clothes for each other. Then they talk dirty on IM like they're having sex. They say there's nothing in the Bible that says they can't do what they're doing, and that it's the safest sex anyone can have.
>
> I don't think my girlfriend will go for it, but do you think I should ask? What *does* the Bible say about cybersex? —*Virtually yours in Denver*

Response:

I'm hearing both uncertainty and curiosity in your voice. When you say, "I don't think my girlfriend will go for it," you need to trust your instincts. The two of you, no doubt, have a great relationship. She wants to keep the physical aspect of your relationship pure for marriage.

While your friends describe what they're doing as "safe," I believe they're walking down a dangerous road. I'm guessing once a couple starts talking dirty to each other and removing clothes, they will probably eventually come to the point when they'd want to get to the next level. That level would probably happen in 3-D and would be less safe since they've been tempted with some very real images of each other.

I personally believe your relationship would be damaged if you were to frame it like a pornographic website. Watching your girlfriend remove her clothes on the Internet doesn't respect her. You need to respect your girlfriend and she needs to respect you. When she puts herself on display for you, you are sapping the intimacy right out of your relationship.

And I've got news for you about your girlfriend, too, my brother. Most women aren't wired to sit and watch their man undress. It's all about feeling safe and secure with you that she loves.

It's true that the Bible has nothing specifically to say about cybersex— just like it has nothing specific to say about X-rated chat rooms, pirating DVDs, or popping Ecstasy. But does that give these activities a stamp of approval from God? Sorry—it doesn't work that way. There are no "six simple rules" for dating in the Bible that tell you it's OK to touch her breast but you're going too far when you watch her get naked on a computer screen. The Bible *does* say sexual intercourse is only for marriage, and you've probably heard that a hundred times from your parents and youth leaders too.

So how far may a boyfriend and girlfriend go? May they hold hands? May they hug? May he put his hand up her shirt? May she touch him through his pants? May they look at each other naked? These are very difficult questions to answer because every relationship is at different stages and the participants have varied backgrounds and ages to consider.

Here's what I learned from a wise man named Walter Trobisch. He takes Genesis 2:24, which we've already looked at, and divides it into three aspects of a relationship. There's "leaving" your parents, which means making the public commitment of marriage. There's "uniting," which is a growing emotional and spiritual intimacy and openness that can only come through real talk and sharing. And there's "one flesh," which is sexual activity leading to and culminating in sexual intercourse in marriage.

All three need to be in balance with each other as a relationship grows. If you move too fast and far along the line of "one flesh" (sexual activity) and leave behind the "uniting" part (emotional and spiritual openness), the relationship gets out of balance. If you get to "one flesh" before the "leaving" (marriage commitment), the relationship is seriously out of whack and out of God's will. And you can be sure that every time you "up" your level of sexual interaction, you find yourself closer to the step of sexual intercourse.

Here's the thing, it's a lot easier to make out and end up in bed than it is to share your lives spiritually and emotionally (especially for guys). But that's where the real work of any relationship is—and the real payoffs. The more time and energy you spend getting united emotionally and spiritually, the healthier your relationship will be now and in the long run.

So, you see, I'm not setting down rules for how far to go and when, except that it's definitely against God's will to have sex without marriage. I want you to have wise guidelines to help you in growing a relationship all the way to marriage and beyond.

Let me be really clear. Sexual intercourse before marriage is wrong! And the emotional consequences of pressuring your girlfriend into intimate situations may surprise you. If you give of yourself sexually, your entire relationship could change in ways you are not prepared for and may regret. If you have an honest and open relationship, you will talk about these things and the long-term consequences that could ensue. —Ron

> Message:
>
> My boyfriend and I have already had sex. We've now done it three times and each time we vow we'll never do it again, but every time we get alone together it's impossible *not* to.
>
> After the last time, I thought I was pregnant since my period was four days late. But then I got it. We haven't had sex since, but I know we will again. I wish I could tell you we were going to get married but we're not even engaged. I'm pretty sure we will get married some time.
>
> I feel guilty for what I've done. My parents would kill me if they knew I was having sex. But at the same time, I feel special that I've shared myself with the guy I love. Is what I've done wrong? I'm worried I will go to hell if I don't marry my boyfriend now that I've had sex with him.
> —Calgary

Response:

I'm glad you took the time to write. You and your boyfriend have made a huge decision to have sex. I think you probably already know that sex before marriage is wrong. Sexual intercourse, a man and a woman becoming one, is only for those who are married. God made that pretty clear in the Bible.

There are a few things that I don't know from your letter. First, I don't know how you and your boyfriend came to the decision to go all the way. While having sex before marriage is wrong, what I say to you depends on just how you made this decision. Second, I don't know if you and your boyfriend feel the same about having sex. It sounds to me like you have some reservations, but I'm not sure about your boyfriend.

Both of you have made vows not to have sex again, but neither of you seems strong enough to show the restraint necessary to keep that promise. I'm not sure how strong your relationship is at this point since you said "I'm pretty sure" we're going to get married. At the end of your letter you said you're worried you might go to hell if you don't marry your boyfriend.

Personally, I'm not convinced the two of you are marriage-bound, and I'm wondering, given your uncertainty, whether you and your boyfriend have even talked about getting married. I have a couple of huge concerns. One is that it sounds like you are having unprotected sex. The second is that you are not using birth control.

Saying you thought you might be pregnant tells me you are having unprotected sex. This brings me to a dilemma: I believe having sexual intercourse before marriage is 100 percent wrong and that it goes against what God wants in your relationship, but I also think you need to be safe. If you haven't talked with your boyfriend about marriage or sexual intercourse, I'm guessing you haven't talked about sexually transmitted diseases or pregnancy.

So here's my advice. Ask for forgiveness and put the brakes on having sex. If you don't, you are setting yourself up for some long-term consequences, sister. One is the possibility of contracting a sexually transmitted disease such as herpes. The second is that you and your boyfriend could easily end up as teenage parents. That would affect the lives of many people you probably haven't even stopped to consider besides you and your boyfriend: the baby, your friends, your parents, your brothers and sisters, your grandparents, and your college admissions counselor, who was really looking forward to meeting you.

Let me repeat: you and your boyfriend should not be having sex. *But if you are, you need to use a condom, pure and simple.* You can go to your doctor, school nurse, or school guidance counselor for help on this issue. Some of you, dear readers (and your parents), will be floored that I would give you that kind of advice. My response is that it would be irresponsible *not* telling you to use protection.

But I also have to tell you that there are ways for you and your boyfriend to stop having sex. Tell someone you trust about your struggles. If you two *really* want to go back to a chaste relationship, you need accountability partners who will ask you if you are having sex.

While you can never undo the emotional surrender you have given over to your boyfriend, and physically you will never be a virgin again, you *can* do what many teens are doing, and that is "reclaiming your virginity." Some people call it "second generation virginity." The two of you pledge not to have sex again until you get married and stay true to your promise.

Here's how it works. The two of you sit at a computer and draft a "pledge form" in which you promise to stop having sex. Then both of you should sign it. I know it's difficult (believe me I *do* know it's difficult!). You will find yourselves alone, aroused, and wanting to have sex so bad you feel like you just can't help it. But you and your boyfriend have to help each other, and one of you has to stop what you're doing when you get to the point of wanting to take off your underwear. It's as simple as that.

Having sex before marriage is a sin, and sin separates us from God. Isaiah 59:2 says, "But your iniquities have separated you from your God; your sins have hidden his face from you, so that he will not hear." But the good news is, when you confess your sin, God will forgive you in the same way he forgives any other sin you confess. And God's Spirit will help you to resist the temptation to keep on sinning.

When you help each other and hold one another accountable, your relationship should grow even stronger. One day, when you do get married, you can have all the sex you want. And it will be great—and right with God. —*Ron*

OK, it's time to log off. I want to thank those who sent me these questions. For those who have more questions, I encourage you to ask your youth pastor, your guidance counselor, your parents or older siblings, or older couples who are mentors to you.

And don't forget, you and your partner can pray together about your struggles. When you include God in your relationship, good things happen. It's the only love triangle you should ever find yourself in! Ecclesiastes 4:12 says "Though one may be overpowered, two can defend themselves. A cord of three strands is not quickly broken." Together, you and your partner may be able to overcome a lot of your difficulties with honesty, respect, and good communication. And with God in your relationship, you will not be broken.

CHAPTER 10
Laura King Live, Part 1

Hey, reader. I thought for this chapter we could watch a TV show together. You've probably seen *Larry King Live* on CNN—you know, the guy with the deep, resonant voice, big glasses, and suspenders who interviews important people? You may not know that Larry has a third cousin three times removed named Laura King. Amazingly, she has her own TV show! And here's a real coincidence: all this week her topic has been teens, sex, and relationships.

Laura King: Good evening, America. Welcome back to *Laura King Live.* . . . All week we've been looking at teens and sex, covering topics from premarital sex to date rape to the recipe for successful relationships. Last night, we talked about celibacy for teens.

Tonight we'll explore the special challenges faced by gay teens. We're joined by Steve Teller from Boone, North Carolina; Jocelyn Reinhart from Toronto, Ontario; and Kristyn Chan from Los Angeles, California. Later in the show we'll be joined by Pastor Mark Keller and youth counselor Kelly Singh.

Steve, let's start with you. When did you first realize you were gay?

Steve: Well, I always knew I was different. I remember from a very early age being attracted to other boys. It wasn't a sexual thing. I just gravitated to guys—liked being around them. It's not like you go home at night and say, "I must be gay." You just accept who you like and who you don't.

But to answer your question, when I got to be a teenager, I realized I had no interest in girls, if you know what I mean. I had lots of friends who were girls, but I had no "feelings" for girls. Most of my friends were pairing off and having on-again-off-again relationships, but I wasn't one of them. I found myself having crushes on male teachers and other guys in my classes.

Laura King: Jocelyn, when did you know you were a lesbian?

Jocelyn: I guess I knew I was different from my friends from the time I was way young. Like many girls, I didn't feel comfortable with the normal girl stuff. I hated dresses; I hated girly things in general. That doesn't make someone a lesbian, of course, but that's what I was feeling. I didn't *feel* like a girl. I now know that realizing this was just the beginning of my journey of discovery.

Laura: What does that mean, you didn't *feel* like a girl? Did you feel like a boy?

Jocelyn: (*Laughs.*) No, not like a boy. But maybe something in between. When I was twelve, I kissed another girl at a sleepover. I felt ashamed, of course. I grew up being taught homosexuality was wrong so I felt very guilty. But I was excited, too, because it felt right to me. It was a major point in my discovery.

Laura: Does it feel right to you, Steve?

Steve: I can sit here and tell you it feels right because I now know I'm gay, but I was raised by parents and older brothers who had lots of words for gay guys. Not nice words. It's been very difficult.

Laura: When did you tell your parents?

Steve: I didn't tell them. My mom asked me. She came into my bedroom and asked me all kinds of questions. My dad has never said a word about it to me, but my parents tell each other everything so I know he knows.

Laura: Do your parents know, Jocelyn?

Jocelyn: Yes.

Laura: How did they react?

Jocelyn: Well, my mother told me it was just a phase I was going through, and if I prayed hard about it, I could be cured.

Laura: Did you pray?

Jocelyn: I did! I grew up thinking that being homosexual was unnatural, something from the devil. There are Bible passages that say same-sex relationships are wrong. It's very hard.

Laura: How do you know you're gay?

Jocelyn: I just feel closer to girls. I trust them and want to be physically close to them too. But it's more than that, Laura. It's not only about being physical. I connect with girls on a much more intimate level than I ever could with a guy. I've never actually had a relationship with a girl. I think in the back of my mind I feel like one day I'll wake up and like guys or something. But then I wake up every day and that's *not* the way I feel.

Laura: What's it like being a gay teen, Steve?

Steve: People always said stuff to me when I was younger. They called me "fairy" and "fag" and "girly-man" and stuff like that. Bullying stuff. Straight guys get that too, if they're quiet or skinny or something.

When I became a teen and told people—that's when things got crazy. People are scared of you in a weird way. Teachers and guys, especially. Not girls. Girls are great. They always seem to understand stuff like that. But I don't care what anyone thinks. It's who I am, Laura. I can't change it. I was born this way and there's nothing I can do to change how I feel.

Laura: Jocelyn, Christians say being gay is wrong. Only heterosexual relationships are OK. Is the Bible wrong?

Jocelyn: Laura, I believe the Bible is God's Word. I'm a believer and I love Jesus. I struggle with what is right, but I don't know how I can change how I feel. I ask God why I was born feeling this way and how it could be wrong. I don't know why it's wrong that two people can't openly love each other if they are the same gender. It's hard. There aren't a whole lot of people to talk to about it.

Laura: We've got Pastor Mark Keller and youth counselor Kelly Singh via satellite from Eastwood College in Nebraska. Pastor Keller, *is* homosexuality wrong?

Mark: Well, Laura, Christians are divided on that question. Some say a sexual relationship should only be between a man and a woman, and that this union should only occur after they are married. Others condemn homosexuality *and* people who are homosexuals.

There are also Christians who believe that homosexuality is a sin, but at the same time, homosexuals, like everyone else, are created and loved by

God. They distinguish between the act of homosexuality and the homosexual person.

And still others believe that gay and lesbian people were created as homosexuals, and it's OK for them to live in a committed, monogamous relationship.

Laura: What do you believe, Pastor Keller?

Mark: I struggle with this question, Laura. All people are God's people. All people are sinners. The apostle Paul says in 1 Timothy 1:10 and in 1 Corinthians 6:9 that practicing homosexuality is a sin. In the same verse he says lying and committing adultery is also a sin. But is one sin greater than another? Is homosexuality a greater sin than, say, lying? Many Christians think it is and take it a step further by condemning a person who is homosexual. That's wrong. Jesus said that he who is *sinless* may cast the first stone. Christians (who certainly aren't sinless!) cast a lot of stones at gays and lesbians.

Laura: But is homosexuality a sin?

Mark: I believe homosexuality wasn't part of God's plan for men and women—it's one of the things that came into the world after the fall. Paul says the *practice* of homosexuality is wrong. That's an important word—practice. Many Christians are homosexuals but do not act on their desires—they remain single and celibate.

Here's the tough reality. As I've just said, the Bible clearly teaches that homosexual practice is wrong. So my church teaches that, just as single people are called to refrain from having sex, homosexuals are too. That's really hard to live out, I know. And because the church recognizes how hard it is, they've made a point of saying that Christians ought to support and love their gay brothers and sisters in Christ—to exercise the same compassion for them as they struggle with obeying Christ as they do for any other people.

I guess what I'm trying to say is, sin is sin—and we're not to treat homosexual sin as a greater wrong than any other kind of sin. It's important to remember that Christians who are homosexuals are full members of the church community, and they're called to serve in the church just as heterosexuals do. Sometimes they sin, just like we all do, and then they need to repent and know that God forgives them.

Laura: Kelly Singh . . . you deal every day with teenagers who are gay.

Kelly: Laura, I just want to piggyback on your earlier question about how a teen knows he or she might be gay or lesbian. I explain it this way: whichever gender makes you tingle, you can trust that is who you are attracted to. It's as simple as that. And then to piggyback on Pastor Mark's statement that if you are born with this tingle, how can you simply ignore it?

Laura: Do teens have a rough time when they realize they are gay or lesbian?

Kelly: I can tell you that gay teens have high suicide rates and high rates for depression. Everything around them says you aren't normal if you are gay. Your parents might not speak to you, or, like Jocelyn's mother, they might tell you that you will be cured if you pray, as if you have a dreaded disease. But the tingle remains. Often teens think the only answer is to commit suicide, which is very sad, Laura. I can't believe that's what God wants.

Laura: Is homosexuality wrong, Kelly?

Kelly: I'm a Christian, Laura. I love Jesus. I also love the kids I counsel who are gay and lesbian. And I know God loves them too. I haven't sorted it out enough to give you a straight answer. I know that's the easy answer, but many Christians who deal with teens who are homosexual or with parents whose kids are gay or lesbian will tell you the same thing. Like Mark, I believe in the Bible. But I'm still not clear on how to interpret it on homosexual issues.

Laura: I want to thank all of you for coming on the show tonight. I hope you can join us again for tomorrow night's show when we look at kids who have a completely different challenge. Tune in again tomorrow night for our show "Teens with Disabilities: Seeing Past the Wheelchair. . . ."

CHAPTER 11
Laura King Live, Part 2

Hey reader, we're back for another session of *Laura King Live* on CNN.

Laura: Good evening, America, and welcome to tonight's show. If you're joining us for the first time this week, you should know that we're wrapping up another in our week-long series on teens and sex. Tonight's topic is "Teens with Disabilities: Seeing Past the Wheelchair. . . ."

Kids with disabilities live in a world where able-bodied teens rule. The media presents the ideal teen as quarterback, cheerleader, or just the cool guy striding down the hall with his backpack slung low.

But what if you're a teen who opens his locker from a wheelchair or who stays home from the prom because she thinks nobody will dance with a girl who is visually impaired? With me tonight is Zack Smith from South Bend, Indiana, and Kristyn Chan from Los Angeles, California. Zack has been in a wheelchair since a spinal-cord injury that happened when he was eleven; Kristyn has been visually impaired since birth.

Thank you both for coming on the show. Zack, I hear you were going to play for the Irish when you got to college?

Zack: I was going to be running back.

Laura: Tell us about your injury.

Zack: I was with my family at our cottage on Lake Michigan. My brothers and cousins and I always jumped off the rocks at Henry's Peak. I dove into the water and hit a rock. I cracked my spine, and now I'm paralyzed from the waist down. I've been in a wheelchair for five years.

Laura: And Kristyn. You've been blind since birth.

Kristyn: My vision is 80 percent impaired. I need to use a guide dog.

Laura: Both of you go to regular school and do all the things any teen does, right?

Zack: Obviously I'm not going to be a running back, but I pretty much do the things any other kid does. Sometimes people will think I'm different because of the chair I guess. But I'm not. Hey, I argue with my parents as much as my brothers do; I hate doing homework; and I play video games till way after midnight. Like I said, about the only difference between me and my friends is this chair.

Kristyn: I go to regular school too, but I get resource help when I need it. All my stuff is recorded on CD and I have people scribe for me in class, and that gets put on CD too. Because my vision is so limited, I don't always see what's going on. I can go to a volleyball game, but someone has to tell me what's happening. I eat lunch in the courtyard and fill a tray in the cafeteria, but someone has to tell me what's on the sandwiches. I won't let my disability stop me from doing stuff though. Even dancing—I love dances!

Laura: Do you date?

Kristyn: (*Laughs.*) When I was fourteen and fifteen I had a couple of dates—nothing major. The guys I dated were really great, but after a couple of dates, when a boyfriend and girlfriend might start to get kind of serious, it usually ends. When you have a disability, you're always kind of distrustful—like you think maybe someone is going out with you because they feel sorry for you. My mom said I'd just *know* when the right person comes along.

I've had a boyfriend for four months. We started going out in the fall of our senior year. He's great. We talk and talk. I can't tell you what he looks like—except what he's told me and what my friends have told me. We have a normal relationship—it's just that I can't see him.

Laura: Zack?

Zack: For me, it's a bit harder. A chair isn't exactly a chick magnet, you know. It used to bother me a lot when I was younger. Who would go out with someone in a chair? But I've had three girlfriends who are amazing. If someone comes along who I fall in love with, there's no stopping love—that's what my dad says. If not, I'm cool with that. I study hard, have lots of great friends—both guys and girls—and have a great time. It just happens to be from a chair. But if you think about it, most people are sitting in a chair 75 percent of their lives!

Laura: Can you father a child?

Zack: I'm paralyzed from the waist down so people assume I don't have any, uh, function, but I do. I mean . . . I can. It just takes more effort, but that's the fun part! And another thing is that even though my body doesn't do what I want it to, I still have all the normal feelings of every other guy in high school. I get turned on in the same way by the same things as other guys, but I have to use my mind a little more. (Too much information, huh? I have these talks all the time with my rehab trainer.)

Laura: What do you look for in a girl, Zack?

Zack: She has to be hot, of course. Not Paris Hilton hot or anything, but nice looking. I do have standards! And she has to have big dreams like me. I want to be a teacher after college. I love kids.

She has to be funny and nice to all kinds of people—not just the plastic people you see walking around a high school. You know, the ones who look right through you when you're rolling down the hall toward them? She has to be able to talk like crazy because I do. Because sex will be different for the two of us, she'll have to be creative to connect with me. Big ideas and analyzing stuff like movies and TV shows is a must.

Laura: Kristyn, what do you see in a guy?

Kristyn: Well, unlike most girls, looks really don't matter to me! He has to be clean, though. (*Laughs.*) And I do trust my friends if someone isn't a good match for me visually.

Umm, he has to be a good listener. I have to trust him big time. Imagine walking through the dark with someone—you have to trust that person. It's something you feel and know very quickly. I'm very trusting, but I have to be careful that I don't find myself in situations where I could be at a disadvantage.

Laura: Do either of you ever get mad or say, "Why me?"

Zack: I won't lie to you. There are lots of days when I don't want to get out of bed in the morning. It's very hard. Not just the getting around thing—that's OK. I'd do anything to spend one practice in uniform, you know? I'd do anything to run out of the house in the morning, yell good-bye to my mother and not wait for a ride with the van. Stupid stuff, I guess. It's just the stuff that goes through your mind.

But you get up. I'm one of the managers on the team—I take stats, edit film, stuff like that. I have a very important job on the team. And like I said, I'm going to teach, so I've got to study hard and get good grades. I've got lots of great friends on the team. I party with them and stuff like that. Most days are fine.

Kristyn: I've never known what it's like to see, but I can imagine it must be amazing. I'd like to see my mother's face with complete clarity, then burn it into my mind so I can see her when I hear her voice. But I don't think about it that much. I know it sounds sappy, but I've never asked the question "Why me?" (*Laughs.*) For one thing, my mother would never let me!

If I could see, I don't know if I would have spent the amount of time I do playing cello or writing. I don't know if I'd have Matt as my boyfriend or if I'd have the friends I do now. I grew up believing that everything has a purpose and I don't stop to question God's purpose for my life. You don't stand still when you come to an obstacle; you go over it, around it, or through it. That's another one of my mother's pearls of wisdom!

Laura: Thank you both for sharing a bit of your life with our audience today. That's all we have time for tonight. Tune in to *Laura King Live* tomorrow night for an up-close and personal look at "Teen Sex Parties: When Mom and Dad Aren't Home. . . . ."

Closing Credits

Hey, reader, I'm glad you're back. You gotta love *Laura King Live*. Have you ever seen a woman look so good in suspenders? Rumor has it that Larry, her third cousin three times removed, gave them to her when she graduated from Talk Show School.

Well, here we are at the end of the book. If this were a movie, my voice would be accompanied by the closing credits scrolling up the screen. This would be that interval after the last scene of the movie plays out and before the quiet piano music that tells everyone it's safe to leave the theater without missing anything.

It's the space of time when you might see funny bloopers from the making of the movie. So here goes—a few bloopers showing me writing this book. Here's me spilling coffee all over my laptop during chapter 2. Here's me stubbing my toe on the vacuum cleaner when I walked around the corner early one morning as I set to work on chapter 7. Here's me spelling a word wrong. And here's me spelling it wrong again! And check out this hilarious scene of me forgetting the next sentence—see everyone laughing at me? See me blush!

Seriously, I've enjoyed this time with you. Thanks for inviting me into your home. I hope you found some clarity about sex and relationships. Wherever you are in your personal relationship timeline, know that God has a special place and plan for you. He knows you better than anyone. Better than your boyfriend or girlfriend. Better than your best friend. Better than you know yourself. Keep him in your life and include him in all your relationships.

And be sure to pray about your struggles. God is always listening. Never lose hope about your relationships, no matter how confusing they become. God's plan may be different from yours. Listen for his whispers so you can say, along with the psalmist of Psalm 139: "You have searched me, LORD, and you know me. . . . You perceive my thoughts from afar. . . . You are familiar with all my ways. . . . You created my inmost being; you knit me together in my mother's womb. I praise you because I am fearfully and wonderfully made; your works are wonderful, I know that full well."

You *are* wonderfully made, my brother or sister. I was praying for you before I started writing this book; I prayed for you as I wrote this book; I prayed for you before you started reading this book—and I'm still praying for you. God bless all of your relationships. Enjoy every aspect of them with every part of your being—your mind, your emotions, and your body.

And now it's time for the piano music. You may leave the theater. . . .